WALKING CALIFORNIA'S CENTRAL COAST

Also by John McKinney

A Walk Along Land's End

Other books in the *Walking the West* Series:

Walking California's State Parks

Walking California's Desert Parks

Walking the California Coast

Walking Los Angeles

Walking Southern California

Walking the East Mojave

Walking Santa Barbara

Walking California's Central Coast

A Day Hiker's Guide

John McKinney

HarperSanFrancisco
An Imprint of HarperCollins*Publishers*

Portions of this book have appeared in the author's hiking column in the *Los Angeles Times*.

WALKING CALIFORNIA'S CENTRAL COAST : *A Day Hiker's Guide*.

HarperCollins Web Site: http://www.harpercollins.com

HarperCollins®, ☗®, and HarperSanFrancisco™ are trademarks of HarperCollins Publishers, Inc.

Maps designed by Susan Kuromiya

FIRST EDITION

Library of Congress Cataloging-in-Publication Data:

McKinney, John.
    Walking California's Central Coast : a day hiker's guide /
John McKinney. (Walking the West series)

Includes index.

ISBN 0–06–258636–X (pbk.)

1. Hiking—California—Pacific Coast—Guidebooks. 2. Pacific Coast (Calif.)—Guidebooks. I. Title. II. Series.

GV199.42.C22P3363 1996
796.5'1'09794—dc20   95–51516

96 97 98 99 00 ❖ RRD(H) 10 9 8 7 6 5 4 3 2 1

Contents

California's Central Coast

California's Central Coast is the land the great landscape photographer Ansel Adams called home; the place that inspired John Steinbeck's *Cannery Row* and other novels.

The wild geography of Point Lobos moved landscape artist Francis McComas to call it "the greatest meeting of land and sea in the world." With all due respect to the artist and to the prominent point, many such "great meetings" of shore and sea take place along California's Central Coast, which is best explored on short walks and long.

Some walkers will enjoy meeting up with a colony of boisterous elephant seals at Point Año Nuevo. Others will delight in trekking the trackless Nipomo Dunes. Still others will find inspiration in the redwoods of the Santa Cruz Mountains and Big Sur.

Between the Bay Area and the Southland are four coastal counties—San Mateo, Santa Cruz, Monterey, and San Luis Obispo—that offer some of the most memorable walking in the West.

Political pundits often divide the state in half—Northern California and Southern California—though no two agree about the dividing line. Pundits, politicians, "I Love L.A." boosters, and San Francisco chauvinists take note: the Central Coast is a land, a people, and an outlook all its own. As a walking province, it's second to none.

California's Central Coast shares some of the north's weather—generous rains, frequent fogs—as well as some of the South Coast's sunshine and temperate breezes. The area combines the solemn redwood groves and precipitous coastline associated with the coast north of San Francisco with long crescents of sand and a beach culture associated with the Southland.

But the beauty of the Central Coast lies in the coast itself, not in comparisons with other places. *Walking California's Central Coast* explores that beauty.

For the writer—and for the walker—the Central California Coast is defined as the shoreline that extends from a bit south of San Francisco Bay to a bit south of Morro Bay. It is a land that surprises. I say this with some authority, having walked the entire California coast and written a narrative of my journey, *A Walk Along Land's End: Discovering California's Living Coast* (HarperCollins West, 1995). On my walk I found the North Coast's beauty to be inspiring but not surprising. And I found the South Coast's beach culture to be intriguing but not surprising.

The Central Coast, however, surprises: wildflower-covered bluffs, silver crescents of sand, tall dunes, rich estuaries, and two long coastal ranges—the Santa Cruz Mountains and the Santa Lucia Mountains.

Each year millions of visitors drive through Monterey, Big Sur, and Simeon on scenic Highway 1. The twisting road gives drivers and their passengers visual inspiration from the glorious landscapes and seascapes glimpsed through windshields. But there's so much more to the Central Coast that can't be seen from a car.

A more intimate connection with the coast can be made by walking to and along the shore, getting close-up views of that otter grabbing mussels off the rocks, that cormorant diving for a fish. A little effort yields big rewards: wildflowers, wildlife, and wild beaches hidden from the highway.

The Santa Cruz Mountains and the Santa Lucia Mountains offer the hiker excellent trails and fabulous coastal vistas. The Santa Cruz Mountains extend along the coast from a few miles south of San Francisco to the Pajaro River on the Santa Cruz–Monterey county border some eighty miles to the south. Lower and narrower in the northern reaches, the range is higher, wider, and wilder in the south. The young, geologically active mountains support impressive redwood groves. The delights of hiking the Santa Cruz Mountains include deep, Douglas fir– and redwood-lined canyons, view-filled ridges, and tranquil valleys.

What is popularly known as Big Sur is really the Santa Lucia Mountains, a range extending 90 miles from the Carmel Valley in the north to San Simeon in San Luis Obispo County. Trails probe the headwaters of the Arroyo Seco and the Little Sur and Big Sur rivers, which originate in the Ventana Wilderness. Observant hikers may spot a rare and beautiful spirelike tree, the Santa Lucia fir, that grows only in these mountains. The Santa Lucias also mark the southernmost limit of the magnificent coastal redwood's natural range. Fern-lined canyons, oak-studded potreros, and meadows smothered with colorful Douglas irises, pink owl's clover, and California poppies greet the backcountry traveler.

The Santa Lucias have a little-known and rarely visited southern extension in San Luis Obispo County. One hiker's highlight is the 21,678-acre Santa Lucia Wilderness.

San Luis Obispo County also boasts the Irish Hills, which form the inviting backcountry of Montana de Oro State Park. Atop the hills and bluffs grow fields of mustard and poppies that give the park its "Mountain of Gold" name.

A series of nine peaks between San Luis Obispo and Morro Bay originated as volcanoes beneath the sea that covered this area some 15 million years ago. These volcanic rocks, or "morros," include Morro Rock, the famed Gibraltar of the Pacific, as well as several more that are fun to climb: Islay Peak in Montana de Oro State Park, Black Mountain in Morro Bay State Park, and Bishop Peak on the outskirts of San Luis Obispo.

Along with its sandy beaches and dramatic rocky shoreline, the Central Coast boasts several sand dune complexes. Providing a striking backdrop to Monterey Bay's northern beaches are some of the Central Coast's tallest dunes, handsomely shaped mounds inhabited by a number of rare native plants and animals. In the southern part of San Luis Obispo County are the Nipomo Dunes, one of California's largest dune systems. Here great heaps of windswept sand are held in place by ice plant, verbena, grasses, and silver lupine.

Visitors to the Central Coast should not overlook its wetlands: freshwater and saltwater marshes, estuaries, sloughs, and lagoons. Scientists say that a high percentage of all sea life along the Central Coast originates in Morro Bay Estuary. The triangular-shaped marsh, lined with eelgrass and pickleweed, is an important spawning and nursery habitat for fish. A walk along the Morro Sand Spit that separates Morro Bay from the ocean is one to remember.

Elkhorn Slough, the largest wetland between Morro and San Francisco bays, is a critical rest stop and feeding ground for tens of thousands of migratory birds. Bird-watchers flock to Elkhorn Slough, where the record was established for the most bird species sighted in a single day—116, no less!

The Central Coast offers much wildlife to watch. In autumn, monarch butterflies cluster in the eucalyptus in Montana de Oro State Park and in the Monterey pines of San Simeon State Park. The eucalyptus grove at Natural Bridges State Beach hosts the largest gathering of monarch butterflies in America.

Truly enormous elephant seals (males reach lengths of sixteen feet and weigh three tons) arrive at Año Nuevo Point in December and come ashore to breed. Walkers are treated to a wildlife drama that attracts visitors from all over the world—a closeup look at the largest mainland population of elephant seals.

Much of the Central Coast's offshore waters are part of a designated sea otter refuge. Otters can often be seen bobbing in the surf or floating on their backs. During the winter months, migrating California gray whales can be viewed from many places along the Central Coast.

In addition to abundant natural attractions, many Central Coast walks have great historical or cultural interest. Hearst Castle (Hearst San Simeon State Historical Monument) offers four fabulous walking tours of the palatial estate of the late newspaper tycoon William Randolph Hearst.

A walk through Old Monterey explores early California's first capital, the once-bustling sardine trade on Cannery Row, and the underwater world revealed at the famed Monterey Bay Aquarium. If you want to take a walk on the wild side of a college campus, hike Pogonip Park next to the University of California at Santa Cruz or Poly Canyon alongside California Polytechnic State University at San Luis Obispo.

Central Coast residents have been, and are, enthusiastic trail boosters. During one weekend in 1969, dedicated members of the Sempervirens Fund and the Santa Cruz Trails Association turned out more than 2,000 volunteers to dig, clear, prune, and otherwise improve the Skyline to the Sea Trail. Area volunteers also put together an annual Trails Day that became a model for organizations throughout the state and across the nation.

In Santa Cruz, city planners, conservationists, and trail groups are at work building a path that will circle the city. San Luis Obispo County has an ambitious Trails Plan that calls for linking existing trails through agricultural lands and for connecting the city of San Luis Obispo with the beach to the west and Los Padres National Forest to the east.

California's Central Coast has long been recognized as something special and efforts made to secure its protection go way back. In 1902 the California state park system was born with the establishment of the California Redwood Park at Big Basin Redwoods State Park in Santa Cruz County. Californians successfully preserved many more "redwood parks" during the twentieth century, but the redwoods at Big Basin remain one of the gems of the state park system.

Big Sur began receiving some measure of federal protection in 1906 when it became part of the Monterey National Forest. Much of today's Monterey District of Los Padres National Forest is composed of two wilderness areas—the Ventana Wilderness and the Silver Peak Wilderness.

California's Central Coast, once simply considered a land situated between North and South, has become a destination in itself—ready to be explored, discovered, and enjoyed by the walker who appreciates natural beauty, small-town life, and one of the world's great meetings of land and sea.

Acknowledgments

The author would like to express his sincere appreciation for the expertise offered during the preparation of this guide by the U.S. Forest Service, particularly representatives in the Santa Lucia and Monterey district offices, as well as the California Department of Parks and Recreation, the San Mateo County Park and Recreation Department, and the San Luis Obispo County Department of Parks and Recreation. A special thank you goes to the many rangers, superintendents, and office and field personnel who care for California's Central Coast, and who so courteously field- and fact-checked the information in this guide.

Walking California's Central Coast

The Central Coast parks are grouped by geography into chapters, then further organized in roughly north-to-south order. Most of the parks clearly belong in their respective categories, but I've made judgment calls on where to place a couple of parks that straddle geographical areas. For example, Wilder Ranch State Park is in the foothills of the Santa Cruz Mountains. Should the park be included in the Santa Cruz Mountains chapter or the Santa Cruz coast chapter?

For each destination, I briefly mention **Terrain** and **Highlights,** followed by **Distance,** expressed in round-trip mileage figures. The hikes in this guide range from 1 to 15 miles, with the majority in the 5- to 8-mile range. Gain or loss in elevation follows the mileage.

Degree of Difficulty is provided to help you match a walk to your ability. You'll want to factor in both mileage and elevation as well as trail conditions, terrain, and season. Hot, exposed chaparral or miles of boulder-hopping can make a short walk seem long.

Hikers vary greatly in relative physical condition, but you may want to consider the following: an easy walk suitable for beginners and children would be less than 5 miles with an elevation gain of less than 700 or 800 feet. A moderate walk is one in the 5- to 10-mile range, with under 2,000 feet of elevation gain. You should be reasonably fit for these. Preteens sometimes find the going difficult. Hikes of more than 10 miles and those with more than a 2,000-foot gain are for experienced hikers in top form.

Season is the next item to consider. California's Central Coast offers four-season hiking. Almost all the trails in this guide are accessible year-round, but the heat of summer and the heavy rains of winter may prevent you from having a pleasant walk.

Precautions have been noted in some cases. For example, a few trails in this guide may be impassable in winter and spring because of high water. Relevant fire and flood information has also been included.

An introduction to each walk describes what you'll see in a particular park, preserve, or forest area, and what you'll observe along the trail: plants, animals, panoramic views. You'll also learn about the geologic and human history of the region.

The **Directions to trailhead** take you from the nearest major highway to trailhead parking. For trails having two desirable trailheads, directions to each are given. A few trails can be walked one way, with the possibility of a car shuttle. Suggested car-shuttle points are noted.

After the directions to the trailhead, you'll read a description of **The walk**. Important junctions and major sights are pointed out, but I've left for you to discover the multitude of little things that make a hike an adventure.

Options allow you to climb higher or farther or take a different route back to the trailhead.

On the Trail

Choose the pace that's best for you. Rest once an hour for a few minutes. To keep your momentum and to avoid stiffness, it's better to take several short rests rather than one long one. Set a steady pace, one you can keep up all day. Wear a watch, not because you have an appointment with a waterfall and must be punctual, but because a watch gives you some idea of pace and helps you get back to the trailhead before dark.

Walking uphill takes energy. Walking 2 miles an hour up a 10 percent grade requires as much energy as hiking 4 miles an hour on level trail. Climbing can be especially difficult at high altitudes.

Many people prefer walking solo, but having two or three in your party is a definite advantage: if something goes wrong, someone can go for help. Hiking with a group is a good idea for first-time walkers.

Alas, backcountry travelers are not always immune from urban attitudes, stresses, and crimes. While most of our state parks are far safer than our urban environment, walkers—particularly women walkers—must be aware that unsavory characters are not unknown on the trail. Your "street smarts" coupled with your trail sense are two keys to avoiding trouble.

Sometimes, after a few hikes, a craving for solitude develops—by which time you should be able to take care of yourself on the trail. There's a lot to be said for solitary hiking, as the writings of Thoreau, Whitman, and Muir would seem to indicate.

Walking Hints

Many day hikes require little more equipment than comfortable shoes, yet hikers often overburden themselves with such nonessentials as hunting knives, hatchets, and propane stoves. The idea with equipment is to take only what you need. You want to get so comfortable with your equipment that you don't think about it; what little you need is on your back and what you don't need is far away.

Footwear: Day hiking begins and ends with the feet. If you're carrying a day pack over easy terrain you don't need a heavy pair of boots. Running shoes or walking shoes can even serve to get you started. But if you do much hiking over rough terrain, a good pair of boots is necessary and well worth the money. A lightweight pair with a Vibram sole will do nicely. Don't buy more boot than you need. A number of fine walking shoes and running shoe–hiking boot combinations on the market will give you miles of comfortable walking.

Blisters can ruin any hike, so be sure to break in your boots before you hit the trail. Walk around town until your feet develop a callous indifference to your boots.

Clothing: You probably have most of what you need in your closet.

A T-shirt layered with a button-down cotton shirt gives you lots of temperature-regulating possibilities. Add a wool shirt and a windbreaker with a hood and you'll be protected against sudden changes in temperatures.

Shorts are useful much of the year in Southern California, and in many places in the Central and Northern regions. Test your shorts by stepping up on a chair. If they pull around the groin, butt, or thigh, they're too tight.

For cooler days or walking through brush, a sturdy pair of long pants is necessary.

Hats prevent the brain from frying and protect from heat loss when it is cold.

Sunglasses are a big help when walking along Central Coast beaches or across hot, exposed coastal slopes. Make sure you buy a pair that provides UV protection.

Food: On a day hike, weight is no problem, so you can pack whatever you wish. Remember to pack out what you pack in. The day you hike is not the day to diet. There's a lot of calorie burning on a hike and quite an energy cost. You'll need all your strength, particularly on steep grades. Gorp, or trail mix, with dried fruit, nuts, raisins, and M&M's, is high-octane fuel. A sandwich, fruit, and cookies make a good lunch. Avoid a big lunch. Exertion after a big lunch sets up a competition between your stomach and your legs. Your legs lose, and you may develop weakness and indigestion.

Water: It's still possible to drink from some backcountry streams and springs without ill effect, but each such water source should be carefully scrutinized. I highly recommend that you do not drink untreated water in any Central Coast park, preserve, or national forest.

Many hikers assume that water is pure, and 48 hours later develop a queasy conviction that their assumption was wrong. Water may harbor the *Giardia lamblia* organism, one of the causes of "traveler's diarrhea." When you approach that stream, Sierra cup in hand, think about what may be upstream. A campground? Cows? High-rushing mountain streams are usually safer than stagnant ponds. Bring purification tablets and/or a filter and use them if you have the slightest doubt about water quality.

First-Aid Kit: Carry a standard kit supplemented with an Ace bandage in the event of hiker's knee or a sprained ankle. Take moleskin for blisters. Insect repellent won't stop mosquitoes from buzzing around but it will inhibit their biting.

Day Pack or "Summit Pack": A day pack is a soft, frameless pack that attaches to your shoulders and sometimes includes a hip band or waist belt for support. A good one will last a lifetime. Those thin cotton or nylon bike bags and book bags won't hold up well. Shoulder pads are a nice feature in a day pack. You'll only be carrying 5 or 10 pounds, but the pads are comfortable on a long hike. Get a pack with a tough covered zipper. Double-O rings slip and aren't the greatest shoulder-strap adjusters. Get tabler buckles; they don't slip and they adjust quickly.

Precautions

We still react instinctively when we feel threatened by some aspect of the natural world. Don't let the few biters, stingers, and hazards mentioned below make you apprehensive about going into the backcountry.

Blisters: There's nothing worse than walking on feet that burn like hot coals. To avoid blisters, make sure your boots fit properly. Keep pulling up your socks and see to it that they don't bunch up. Act quickly if you feel a blister developing. Cut a hole in moleskin a little larger than your red spot and stick it in place with the blister poking through the hole. The idea is to surround it so the boot can't get at it. (If you covered it you could irritate it further, and you'd have to peel the tape off the blister. Ouch!) Some hikers put a double layer of tissue paper over the blister and fasten the tissue in place with surgical tape. If you get a full-grown blister, pop it with a clean needle inserted under the edge, apply antiseptic, and put moleskin over the area.

Poison Oak: This infamous plant grows abundantly throughout

California mountains up to an elevation of 5,000 feet. It's a sneaky devil. It may lurk under other shrubs or take the form of a vine and climb up a redwood. The leaves are 1 to 4 inches long and glossy, as if waxed.

All parts of the plant at all times of the year contain poisonous sap that can severely blister skin and mucous membranes. Its sap is most toxic during spring and summer. In fall, poison oak is particularly conspicuous; its leaves turn to flaming crimson or orange. However, since its color change is more a response to heat and dryness than to season, its "fall color" can occur anytime in California. Leaves on some plants can be turning yellow or red while plants in most spots are putting out green leaves. In winter, poison oak is naked, its stalks blending into the dull hue of the forest.

Contrary to popular belief, you can't catch it from someone else's rash, nor from oozing blisters, but petting an animal or handling a piece of clothing that carries it can make you a victim.

There are a multitude of remedies. Perhaps most common is the regular application of calamine lotion or cortisone cream. If you're particularly sensitive to poison oak, always wash thoroughly immediately after a hike, using cold water and a basic soap such as laundry detergent. Launder your hiking clothing separately as soon as possible. A dip in the ocean can help; a few tablespoons of baking soda added to a tub of lukewarm water calms the itchies as well. You organic types will probably want to pick some mugwort, an effective panacea. Its fresh juice applied directly to the pained area relieves itching.

Rattlesnakes: Sometimes rattlesnakes take to the trail to enjoy the sunshine, so keep an eye out. Despite the common fear of rattlers, few people see them and rarely is anyone bitten. Only a small percentage of bites cause serious injury.

The red diamond rattlesnake is found in coastal, hill, and desert regions. The sidewinder and Western diamondback inhabit the desert, and the Southern Pacific rattler lives in coastal regions.

If you've been bitten, remain calm. Check to be sure you've actually been envenomized. Look for swelling around the wound within 5 minutes. If it doesn't swell, you've probably escaped and may not require hospital treatment. If swelling and other symptoms occur—numbness around the lips or hairline, a metallic taste in the mouth, or twitching facial muscles—it got you and you need immediate treatment.

Getting to a hospital emergency room is more important than any other first aid. Keep the site of the wounds as immobilized as possible and relax. Cutting-and-suction treatments are now medically out of vogue and advised only as a last resort if you're absolutely sure you can't get to a hospital within 4 hours.

Bees: More fatalities occur from allergic reactions to insect stings than from rattlesnake bites. People allergic to bee stings can get a desensitization shot and a specially equipped bee kit from an allergist.

Ticks: These insects are ¼ to ½ inch long and about the color of the ground, so they're hard to see. Ticks are usually picked up by brushing against low vegetation. When hiking in a tick area it's best to sit on rocks rather than fallen logs. Check your skin and clothing occasionally. You and your loved one can groom each other like monkeys at the zoo. If one is attached to the skin, it should be lifted off with a slow gentle pull. Before bathing, look for ticks on the body, particularly in the hair and pubic region.

Lyme disease, while rare in California, is the most common tick-carried illness. Symptoms usually include a red, ringlike rash on the skin where the tick attaches itself. The rash is often accompanied by flulike symptoms of headaches, chills and fever, fatigue, and aching muscles. If the disease goes untreated, second-stage symptoms are meningitis and abnormal heartbeat; third-stage symptoms (months or years later) can include arthritis. A blood test can determine if a person is infected. Antibiotics are a very effective treatment.

Getting Lost and Found

Even experienced hikers can get lost. Getting lost is usually the result of taking a "shortcut" off an established trail. The danger is magnified if a hiker ventures out alone or fails to tell anyone where he's gone or when she expects to return.

Try to avoid getting lost in the first place. Know your physical condition and don't overtax yourself. Check your boots and clothing. Be prepared for bad weather. Inquire about trail conditions. Allow plenty of time for your hike, and even more time for your return to the trailhead.

When you're on the trail, keep your eyes open. If you're hiking so fast that all you see is your boots, you're not attentive to passing terrain—its charms or its layout. STOP once in a while. Sniff wildflowers, splash your face in a spring. LISTEN. Maybe the trail is paralleling a stream. Listen to the sound of mountain water. On your left? On your right? Gaze up at that fire lookout on the nearby ridge. Are you heading toward it or away from it? LOOK AROUND. That's the best insurance against getting lost.

So you're really lost? Stay calm. Don't worry about food. It takes weeks to starve to death. Besides, you've got that candy bar in your day pack. You have a canteen. And you have a poncho in case of rain. You're in no immediate danger, so don't run around in circles like a mindless chicken.

LOOK AROUND some more. Are there any familiar landmarks in sight? Have you been gaining elevation or losing it? Where has the sun been shining? On your right cheek? Your back? Retrace your steps, if you can. Look for other footprints. If you're totally disoriented, keep walking laterally. Don't go deeper into the brush or woods. Go upslope to get a good view, but don't trek aimlessly here and there.

If it's near dark, get ready to spend the night. Don't try to find your way out in the dark. Don't worry. If you left your itinerary, your rescuers will begin looking for you in the morning. Try to stay warm by huddling against a tree or wrapping yourself in branches, pine needles, or leaves. The universal distress call is three visible or audible signals: three shouts or whistles, three shiny objects placed on a bare summit. Don't build a fire! You could start a major conflagration.

Relax and think of your next hike. Think of the most beautiful place you know—that creek of snowmelt gushing down from that stony mountain, a place where the fish bite and the mosquitoes don't. . . . You'll make it, don't worry.

Backcountry Courtesy

Leave your radio and tape player at home.

Dogs must be kept on a leash at all times and enclosed in a vehicle or tent at night. Dogs are not allowed on trails, or on most beaches. A one-dollar fee is charged for each dog entering a park.

No smoking on trails.

Resist the urge to collect flowers, rocks, or animals. It disrupts nature's balance and lessens the wilderness experience for future hikers.

Litter detracts from even the most beautiful backcountry setting. If you packed it in, you can pack it out.

You have a moral obligation to help a hiker in need. Give whatever first aid or comfort you can, and then hurry for help.

Don't cut switchbacks.

Conservation of Marine Life

Some general rules should be remembered whenever one is observing marine organisms. Rocks that have been turned over should be replaced in their original position; otherwise, the plants and animals originally on the upper surface are now on the bottom and will die; the same, in reverse, holds for animals that were originally on the bottom of the rock.

Whenever digging in sand or mud for clams or other creatures, be sure to shovel the material back into the hole, because many organisms die when their habitat is disturbed. Remember, each species has its own specific habitat, and whenever we disturb its environment, chances are the organism will perish.

1. Santa Cruz Mountains

In 1902 the California state park system was born with the establishment of California Redwood Park in the Big Basin area of the Santa Cruz Mountains. Perhaps it is only fitting that one of the state's proudest possessions—the magnificent redwoods—provided the inspiration for the creation of the Golden State's park system.

In the young, geologically active Santa Cruz Mountains, generous rains support impressive redwood groves, some of which are preserved in state parks: Portola, Henry Cowell Redwoods, and a forest undergoing restoration—the Forest of Nisene Marks. Other redwood groves are preserved in parks administered by San Mateo County and by the East Bay Regional Parks District.

The Santa Cruz Mountains extend some 80 miles along the coast from San Bruno Mountain south of San Francisco to the Pajaro River on the Santa Cruz–Monterey county border. Lower and narrower in its northern reaches, the range is higher, wider, and wilder in the south.

Many of the parks in the Santa Cruz Mountains have excellent trails. Paths, particularly the new Bay Area Ridge Trail, also link parks. The superb Skyline to the Sea Trail links Big Basin Redwoods State Park with Castle Rock State Park and other mountain preserves. This trail—and many local volunteers—made history when the first "Trails Day" ever was held in 1969 to help restore the trail.

Burleigh Murray Ranch State Park
Burleigh Murray Ranch Trail

Terrain: Riparian woodland in valley south of Half Moon
  Bay.
Highlights: Old barn and bridge—glimpse of early ranch
  life.
Distance: To old barn is 2 miles round-trip; to trail's end is
  5 miles round-trip.
Degree of difficulty: Easy to moderate.

Rolling grassland, eucalyptus-grove windbreaks, an old barn and a
bunkhouse—this is ranch country, not the redwood forest typically
associated with the Santa Cruz Mountains.

Beginning in the 1860s, the valley of Mills Creek and surrounding slopes were used for hay growing and cattle grazing. The state
purchased the land in 1983, and the California park service has been
considering a historical emphasis for the state park.

A prized historic structure is the old dairy barn, known as an Eng-
lish bank barn (because it's built into the hillside to facilitate load-
ing from its upper level); such barns are extremely rare in the United
States. Some handsome stonework, rusted farm machinery, and a
1930s ranch house (now the park ranger's residence) add to the rus-
tic scene. The photo opportunities are many on the old ranch.

Meandering through the state park is Mills Creek, named not for
the considerable number of Santa Cruz Mountains sawmills but for
the Mills family, the first owners of the ranch.

The only park trail is the old ranch road that extends from the
park entrance on Higgins Purisima Road some 2 miles northeast.
The path follows Mills Creek to the old barn. Beyond the barn, the
road narrows to a trail; then, beyond some water tanks it fades into
oblivion. (The park service has not yet extended the trail to Skyline
Boulevard.)

Directions to trailhead: From Highway 1, just south of the town
of Half Moon Bay, turn east on Higgins Purisima Road and follow
it 1½ miles to the small parking lot for Burleigh Murray Ranch
State Park on the north side of the road.

The walk: The flat, brush-lined road follows Mills Creek for a ½-
mile before crossing, then recrossing it. A mile out, the road passes

a eucalyptus-shaded picnic site, then angles left past the ranch-house-turned-ranger's-residence, crosses a bridge, and brings you to the large dilapidated barn.

The route beyond the barn is an ever-narrowing footpath through Mills Creek Canyon. At 2 miles, it reaches a trio of leaky water tanks before petering out in thick coastal scrub.

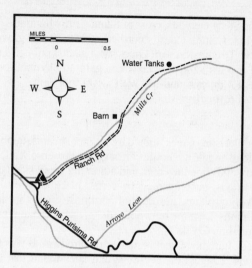

Purisima Creek Redwoods Open Space Preserve

Purisima Creek Trail

Terrain: Steep canyons, crest of Santa Cruz Mountains.
Highlights: Central Coast's northernmost redwood groves.
Distance: To junction with Grabtown Gulch Trail is 2¼ miles round-trip with 200-foot elevation gain; to Skyline Boulevard is 8½ miles round-trip with 1,600-foot gain.
Degree of difficulty: Moderate.

Year-round Purisima Creek, joined by smaller streams, tumbles from Skyline Ridge and flows 3 miles through the preserve. Tall, second-growth redwoods line the creek and adjoining steep-sided canyon.

The redwoods, accompanied by ferns, blackberry bushes, and many flowering plants, are the northernmost groves in the Santa Cruz Mountains. Like the redwoods, the preserve's main trail sticks close to Purisima Creek.

The fate of Purisima Creek's first-growth redwoods was to be cut into shingles. Loggers of the 1860s and later found that the trees were just too big to haul up the steep canyon walls; instead, they sliced the logs into shingles at several canyon mills, then used pack animals to haul the shingles out of the mountains.

Purisima Creek Trail, a county road once upon a time, ascends from the preserve's west entry on Higgins Purisima Road all the way to Skyline Boulevard. The first mile of trail is an easy stroll past some inspiring redwoods. Thereafter the hiking is more difficult.

An option I recommend is the Grabtown Gulch Loop, which adds 4 miles to the hike.

Directions to trailhead: From Highway 1, on the southern outskirts of Half Moon Bay, turn east on Higgins Purisima Road and drive 4½ miles to the parking lot for Purisima Creek Redwoods Open Space Preserve.

The walk: At the signed trailhead, a fire road follows the north side of Purisima Creek, while you join Purisima Creek Trail on the south side. Admiring the second-growth redwoods and the Michael S. Osborn Memorial Grove on the north bank, you ascend moderately with the old road.

A mile's walk brings you to a right-forking pathway; this trail, combined with Grabtown Gulch Trail, reached by continuing a short ¼-mile farther along Purisima Creek Trail, adds a 4-mile loop to your walk.

(Grabtown Gulch Trail ascends very steeply into a ferny gulch, then climbs through a mixed forest of tan oak, madrone, Douglas fir, and young redwoods. You'll loop along the preserve's south boundary near Tunitas Creek Road. This area is believed to have been the site of Grabtown, a way station for teamsters hauling logs to Redwood City. To complete the loop, you'll join the trail descending the ridge west of Grabtown Gulch and return to Purisima Creek Trail.)

Beyond the junction with Grabtown Gulch Trail, Purisima Creek Trail climbs steeply, almost in stair-step fashion, along the creek and in 3 miles reaches Skyline Boulevard.

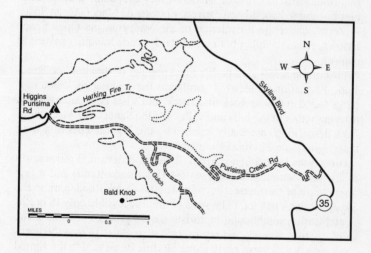

El Corte de Madera
Open Space Preserve
El Corte de Madera Creek Trail

> **Terrain:** High mountain ridge; deep, redwood-lined canyon.
> **Highlights:** Mountain vistas, sandstone formations.
> **Distance:** To Vista Point and Sandstone Formation is 2¼
> miles round-trip.
> **Degree of difficulty:** Easy to moderate.

From its headwaters high on the 2,400-foot ridge traveled by Sky-line Boulevard, El Corte de Madera Creek drops into a deep, Douglas fir– and redwood-lined canyon. El Corte de Madera Open Space Preserve, under the jurisdiction of the Midpeninsula Open Space District, offers the hiker both viewful ridges and tranquil canyons to explore.

Two of the 2,789-acre park's most popular destination are Sand-stone Formation, somewhat similar to the striking rock outcrop-pings found in Castle Rock State Park, and Vista Point, an overlook offering views of the hills and valleys of the Santa Cruz Mountains. Both destinations are easily reached by this leg-stretcher of a walk that begins from Skyline Boulevard.

Directions to trailhead: From Skyline Boulevard, 3 miles north of its intersection with Highway 84 (La Honda Road) and a few miles south of its intersection with Tunitas Creek Road, park in the Skeggs Point Vista lot. (The vista point is accessible only to north-bound traffic; southbound motorists should proceed past the vista, carefully turn around, and return to Skeggs Point.) From the park-ing lot, walk 150 yards north along Skyline Boulevard to the signed entrance for El Corte de Madera Open Space Preserve on the west side of the road.

The walk: Join the dirt road that climbs briefly before descend-ing along El Corte de Madera Creek. You'll see some good-sized firs and second-growth redwoods.

After a mile you'll pass a path leading left to Methuselah Trail-head and very soon reach a second junction.

At this four-way trail intersection, a leftward path goes to Methuse-lah Trailhead.

Make a lazy right to reach Vista Point after a short climb. The vista includes a peak at the ocean and some of the dramatic westward-facing slopes of the Santa Cruz Mountains.

From the four-way trail junction you can also make a sharp right and follow the path ¹⁄₁₀-mile to the preserve's sandstone formations.

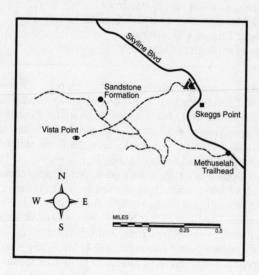

Sam McDonald County Park

Big Trees Trail

> **Terrain:** Redwood grove, meadows.
> **Highlights:** Family-friendly walk in the redwoods.
> **Distance:** 1½ miles round-trip.
> **Degree of difficulty:** Easy.

A thousand acres of redwood forest welcome hikers to Sam McDonald County Park. It's a big welcome indeed because the park adjoins some 9,000 more acres of parkland in Pescadero Creek County Park, Memorial County Park, and Portola State Park. All this parkland—a complex of creeks, canyons, and conifer forests—is laced with miles and miles of trails.

Sam McDonald is a true hiker's park; that is, auto access is limited to the visitor center/ranger station area. Even the park's few campsites are of the walk-in variety. Adding to the hiker-friendly atmosphere is the Sierra Club hikers' hut, a Danish import complete with stove, sleeping quarters, and self-composting toilet.

The park honors Sam McDonald (1884–1957), the son of slaves, who worked his way up from janitor to grounds superintendent at Stanford University. Popular with students, faculty, and administrators, the nature-loving McDonald left his forest property to the university with the stipulation that it be preserved in its wild state. Stanford gave the land to the San Mateo County Parks Department. To learn more about this remarkable man, view the display about McDonald at the park visitor center.

While touring the area, don't miss nearby Heritage Grove, which can be reached by trail from the park or by driving east on Alpine Road a mile from its junction with Pescadero Road.

Sam McDonald Park boasts some inviting trails. McDonald Trail loops 3¹⁄₁₀ miles through a fern-filled redwood forest to the northwest of the visitor center. You can walk to the Sierra Club hikers' hut (3 miles round-trip) and from there follow a path that leads to the awe-inspiring Heritage Grove.

Big Trees Trail is a family-friendly little walk, a taste of the redwood forest. With some creative planning and map reading, you can hike all day—or even a couple of days—through the surrounding redwood parks.

Directions to trailhead: Take La Honda Road (State Highway 84) 8 miles from Highway 1 or 7 miles from Skyline Boulevard to the hamlet of La Honda. Head southeast a short distance on Alpine Road to Pescadero Road. From its junction with Alpine Road, follow Pescadero Road ½-mile west to Sam McDonald County Park.

The walk: From the parking area, cross Pescadero Road and join the fire road. In its initial stages, Big Trees Loop Trail is sometimes the road itself, sometimes the narrow path alongside it.

After ½-mile's climb through second-growth redwoods and some huge stumps, Big Trees Loop Trail begins in earnest among huge primeval redwoods. The path crosses a footbridge over a creek.

A mile from the start, the path begins its descent to Pescadero Road. Cross the road and return to the trailhead.

Portola State Park

Iverson, Summit, Slate Creek Trails

Terrain: A little basin full of redwoods, mixed evergreen forest.
Highlights: Family outing in overlooked park.
Distance: 6 miles round-trip; longer and shorter options possible.
Degree of difficulty: Moderate.

You could call this tranquil park, perched on the opposite side of the Santa Cruz Mountains from nationally renowned Big Basin Redwoods State Park, "Little Basin Redwoods State Park." Like its well-known cousin, this park is a natural basin forested with coast redwoods.

Portola State Park it is, however. Its name honors explorer Don Gaspar de Portola, who led an expedition in search of Monterey Bay (he discovered San Francisco Bay instead) in 1769.

The California landscape has changed immeasurably since Portola's time, but places like Portola State Park still evoke the feeling of wild California. This impression begins outside the park boundaries as you travel Alpine Road. The view is of wide-open spaces, of uncluttered valleys and ridges topped with nothing more than grass and cows.

The state park centers around two creeks—Peters and Pescadero—that meander through a basin. Douglas firs and oaks cloak the ridges while redwoods, accompanied by huckleberry and ferns, cluster in cooler bottomlands.

The redwoods in the area are primarily second-growth trees; this land, like most in the Santa Cruz Mountains, was logged in the nineteenth century. Some large trees, considered unsuitable for timber at that time, escaped the lumbermen's axes and saws and may be seen today inside the park.

The Islam Temple Shrine of San Francisco used the property as a summer retreat for its members from 1924 until the state acquired the land in 1945. During the 1960s, when Pescadero Creek was dammed to provide a large fishing and swimming area, Portola developed an amusement park atmosphere. One year, 150,000 people poured into the small park.

In 1974 the dam was removed and Portola reverted to quieter pursuits—camping, hiking, nature study. Rangers sometimes refer to Portola as a "neighborhood park," meaning that thus far only locals have discovered this ideal-for-a-family-outing small redwood forest.

Fourteen miles of trail loop through the park. My favorite day hike is a 6-mile walkabout that utilizes 5 trails.

Drop in at the park visitor center to view the nature and history exhibits. The park has an active interpretive program with some guided nature walks.

Alas, two park highlights are no more. Magnificent 17-foot-high Shell Tree, almost completely gutted by fire, was a 2,000-year-old redwood that lived on and on—until a careless camper's fire finished it off in 1989. Iverson Cabin, built in 1868 by homesteader Christian Iverson, was a casualty of the 1989 earthquake, and today is little more than a pile of boards.

Directions to trailhead: From Interstate 280 (Junipero Serra Freeway), about 6 miles north of San Jose, exit on Saratoga Avenue and head south, joining Highway 9 in the town of Saratoga. Highway 9 ascends west into the mountains to a junction with Skyline Drive (Highway 35). Turn right (northwest) on Skyline and follow it to a junction with Alpine Road and the signed turnoff to Portola State Park. Turn onto Alpine Road. After 4 miles, turn left on the state park road and continue 3½ miles to the park.

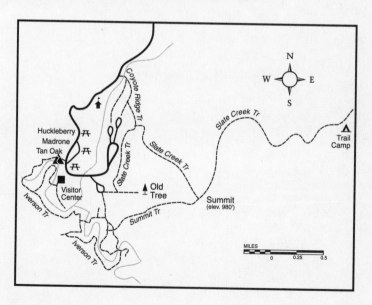

Leave your car at Tan Oak or Madrone picnic areas just across the road from the visitor center.

The walk: Join Sequoia Nature Trail, which begins behind the park visitor center. Tramp through the redwood forest, cross Pescadero Creek, and loop around Louise Austin Wilson Grove, site of the Shell Tree.

Next join Iverson Trail, which meanders along Pescadero Creek. A short side trail leads to diminutive, fern-framed Tip-Toe Falls.

Iverson Trail visits the ruins of Iverson Cabin as it meets a park service road. A right leads to Old Haul Road, which in turn leads 5 miles to San Mateo Memorial County Park. You turn left, cross Pescadero Creek on a bridge, and soon arrive at a signed junction with Summit Trail.

True to its name, Summit Trail ascends some 500 feet in elevation to a (rather undistinguished) summit. It then dips briefly to a saddle and a signed junction with Slate Creek Trail. It's another mile to the park's trail camp, a pleasant, though waterless, rest stop.

From the saddle, Slate Creek Trail descends a pleasant mile west, then contours south to Old Tree Trail and the park's campground. Walk through the campground, then join the park road for the brief return to the park visitor center.

Butano State Park

Mill Ox, Goat Hill, Año Nuevo Trails

Terrain: Redwoods, fern canyon.
Highlights: Mellow hiking, views of coast and Año Nuevo Island.
Distance: 4 miles round-trip with 700-foot elevation gain.
Degree of difficulty: Easy to moderate.

According to Native American lore, *butano* means "a gathering place for friendly visits." Visitors who find out-of-the-way Butano State Park will no doubt agree with this assessment.

On the map, the park seems rather close to the bustling Santa Clara Valley, and to the Bay Area. But this 2,800-acre park, tucked between sharp Santa Cruz Mountains ridges, has a feeling of remoteness that is heightened by a 20-mile trail network leading through redwoods and a fern canyon and climbing to some great vista points.

While most of the redwoods in the park are second-growth, some grand old first-growth specimens remain. The land was logged during the 1880s but did not undergo the devastating clear-cuts common to other coastal ridges of the Santa Cruz Mountains. The steep terrain ruled out conventional transportation, so the woodsmen had to settle for cutting shakes, posts, and fence rails—products that could be more easily hauled to market.

On lower slopes, just above Butano Creek, the walker encounters the forest primeval: redwoods, trillium, sword ferns. Moss-draped Douglas firs, tangles of blackberry bushes, and meadowland are some of the environments visited by the park's diverse trail system. Año Nuevo Vista Point offers fine views of the elephant seal reserve and of the San Mateo coastline.

Directions to trailhead: From Highway 1, turn inland on Pescadero Road and drive 2½ miles to Cloverdale Road. Drive south 3 miles to Butano State Park Road and turn left into the park. Leave your car near the entry kiosk.

The walk: Signed Jackson Flats Trail begins just across from the park entry kiosk. The path starts out in meadowland but soon enters redwoods.

The trail follows the north slope of the canyon cut by Little Butano Creek and reaches a junction with Mill Ox Trail. Take Mill Ox Trail to the right, down to the canyon bottom. Cross Butano State Park Road and join an unmarked (except for an AUTHORIZED VEHICLES ONLY sign) paved road. Ascend through redwoods on this access road. You'll soon reach a junction with Goat Hill Trail, which you follow into a mixed forest of oak and madrone. Stay on this trail to the next intersection: Goat Hill Trail heads left and melts into the woods, but you take the short connector path to Olmo Fire Trail. Turn right. Olmo Fire Trail leads to a junction with Año Nuevo Trail on your left. Take this path over fir- and blackberry bush–covered slopes to Año Nuevo Vista Point, located in a clearing. On clear days, you can look south to Año Nuevo Island, the elephant seal rookery.

From the viewpoint, the trail descends—with enough switchbacks to make a snake dizzy—back to the park entrance.

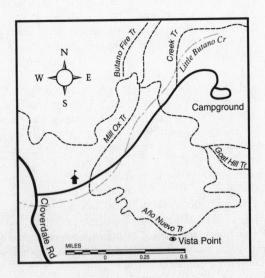

Castle Rock State Park

Saratoga Gap, Ridge Trails

Terrain: Steep slopes with sandstone outcroppings, mixed
evergreen forests, redwood groves.
Highlights: Dramatic rock formations, vistas, waterfall.
Distance: 5½ miles round-trip.
Degree of difficulty: Moderate.
Precautions: Some poison oak; narrow trail on steep slopes
(no place for acrophobes).

Perched high on the western slope of the Santa Cruz Mountains
among frequent fogs (and just above occasional smogs), Castle
Rock State Park offers dramatic rock formations and quiet forest
paths.

Castle Rock, the park's 3,214-foot-high point, is a sandstone formation that appeals to rock climbers, geologists, and photographers. A thick evergreen forest obstructs the view from Castle
Rock. Much better panoramas are to be had atop Goat Rock, a
sandstone outcropping that offers hikers clear-day views of the San
Lorenzo Valley and Pacific Ocean.

At the turn of the century, Castle Rock was already a tourist attraction. InterUrban streetcars carried visitors from the Santa Clara
Valley up to Congress Springs (just above the present-day town of
Saratoga). Intrepid travelers then hiked, or hired a horse and buggy
to carry them, to Castle Rock.

For a pleasant loop through the park, join Saratoga Gap Trail,
which visits Castle Rock Falls and leads to Castle Rock Trail
Camp. Your return is via Ridge Trail, which parallels Saratoga Gap
Trail at higher elevations and offers grand views on clear days.

Directions to trailhead: From Highway 17 just north of Los
Gatos, exit on Highway 9, winding through the town of Saratoga
and ascending the Santa Cruz Mountains to meet Highway 35.
From the junction of Highways 9 and 35 (Skyline Boulevard), drive
south on 35 for 2½ miles to the signed state park lot on the right.
The signed trail begins at the west end of the lot.

The walk: Begin descending on Saratoga Gap Trail in the shade
of oaks and ferns. Soon a side trail offers the opportunity to visit
Castle Rock.

The main path follows a creek and then crosses it on a footbridge. You'll pass a signed trail (your return route) leading to Goat Rock. Continue to Castle Rock Falls, ¾-mile from the trailhead.

Judging by the substantial-looking observation platform, you might expect a more overwhelming spectacle than the 100-foot Kings Creek cascade known as Castle Rock Falls. Ah, but never mind the falls located just up-canyon; take a look down-canyon to the San Lorenzo River watershed and the wide blue Pacific. This view may have been the main reason for the erection of an observation platform.

The path ascends wooded hillsides and, ½-mile beyond the waterfall, leaves behind the trees and climbs into the chaparral. From this elfin forest, hikers get clear-day views of Monterey Bay.

The trail alternates between brushy hillsides and madrone- and oak-filled canyons on the slope of Varian Peak, named for physicist-conservationist Russell Varian, who was instrumental in the creation of the state park.

Russell Point Overlook offers a good view, but a nicer rest or lunch stop is ¼-mile farther at Castle Rock Trail Camp. The camp, located in a knobcone pine forest, has water and picnic tables.

From the camp, you'll retrace your steps as far as the junction with Ridge Trail, which you'll join on an ascent of oak-, madrone-, and boulder-dotted slopes. This path leads a mile to another observation point and to a terrific interpretive center, a collection of outdoor exhibits that really show the lay of the land. (The geography lesson is particularly valuable when fog blankets the Santa Cruz Mountains, as if often does.)

On the final segment of this day hike, you'll loop past Goat Rock, a favorite of local climbers, then descend to rejoin Saratoga Gap Trail. Turn left and return to the trailhead.

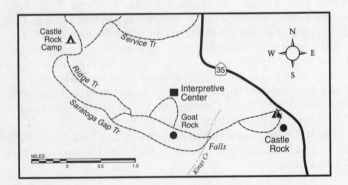

Big Basin Redwoods State Park

Redwood Nature Trail

Terrain: Primeval coast-redwood forest.
Highlights: Park's ancient and impressive redwoods.
Distance: ⅗-mile.
Degree of difficulty: Easy.

For good reason Redwood Nature Trail is the most popular path in the Santa Cruz Mountains: it's an easy tour of some of the tallest, most intriguing redwoods in California. Children particularly like the trail, which is an ideal introduction to the forest for all ages.

Even the most experienced hikers can't help but feel awed by this stand of virgin redwoods—a grove that has inspired millions of visitors since the Big Basin State Park was founded early in the twentieth century.

Individual trees are memorable, too: the giant Father-of-the-Forest, the tall (329 feet high) Mother-of-the-Forest, and the Chimney Tree, which burned from the inside out yet still lives.

Redwood Nature Trail, keyed to an interpretive pamphlet, also explores the lush understory of the 300-foot giants as well as forest ecology from growth to decay.

Directions to trailhead: Well-signed Redwood Nature Trail begins from the Big Basin State Park headquarters area.

Creeping Forest, Big Basin

Creeping Forest, Dool Trails

Terrain: Odd redwood forest.
Highlights: Mellow path among unusual redwoods.
Distance: 2½-mile loop.
Degree of difficulty: Easy.

The oddly angled trees of Big Basin's Creeping Forest are believed to have been pushed into Leaning Tower of Pisa position by a 1952 landslide. Creeping Forest Trail travels slopes forested with redwoods, some growing in their normal perpendicular-to-the-ground fashion, others tilted.

A return route on the opposite side of Redwood Creek utilizes Dool Trail, a path that honors park warden William Dool, who served from 1911 to 1928.

Directions to trailhead: This walk begins near park headquarters.

The walk: From park headquarters, walk west past the campfire circle and cross Opal Creek on a footbridge to the Skyline to the Sea Trail. Head right and hike along Opal Creek, past a junction with Dool Trail (your return route), then across a picnic area to signed Creeping Forest Trail.

The path ascends ½-mile through the redwood forest near Gazo Creek Road. The trail swings west and then south, approaching Gazo Creek Road again before intersecting Dool Trail. Turn south and hike a short mile back to the trailhead.

Pine Mountain

Pine Mountain Trail

Terrain: Pine-clad slopes.
Highlights: Mountain and ocean vistas.
Distance: To Pine Mountain summit is 5 miles round-trip with 1,100-foot elevation gain.
Degree of difficulty: Moderate.

You might not need a break from the magnificent redwoods of Big Basin, but the state park offers one anyway. Pine Mountain Trail leaves the redwoods behind as it ascends slopes of chaparral and knobcone pine.

The trail leads to two viewpoints: Buzzard's Roost, a weathered, windblown, sandstone outcropping offering a panorama of the Santa Cruz Mountains and the sea, and the summit of Pine Mountain itself.

Directions to trailhead: The path begins next to campsite 110 at Bloom Creek Campground.

The walk: Cross the footbridge over Bloom Creek and begin a walk through redwoods. As you pass a junction with East Ridge Trail, your path begins a moderate climb and crosses a road at ¾-mile. As you climb, the vegetation changes from redwoods to tanbark oak to Douglas fir to knobcone pine to ceanothus and manzanita.

Cresting a small ridge, the route contours toward Pine Mountain and, 2 miles from the trailhead, reaches a junction with the summit trail. Leftward is Buzzard's Roost, a short (200-yard) ascent over the sandstone slope. Rightward is the top of Pine Mountain, a ¼-mile climb away.

Berry Creek Falls

Skyline to the Sea, Berry Creek Falls, Sunset Trails

> **Terrain:** Ridges, richly forested canyon.
> **Highlights:** Waterfalls, redwood forest primeval.
> **Distance:** 10½ miles round-trip with 600-foot elevation gain.
> **Degree of difficulty:** Moderate to strenuous.

Tall trees and a trio of waterfalls make this trip through the Big Basin backcountry a hike to remember. The three falls—Berry Creek, Silver, and Golden—are enchanting, as are lesser cascades along Berry Creek.

The walk begins on the Skyline to the Sea Trail but leaves this path well before the sea, detours to visit the waterfalls, then loops back to the main part of Big Basin.

Paths alternate between wet and wild redwood-filled canyons and drier exposed ridges.

This is a grand, clockwise tour of California's first state park, a most memorable walk.

Directions to trailhead: At park headquarters, walk west from the entry-fee kiosk and follow signs for Skyline to the Sea Trail.

The walk: From the Redwood Nature Trail, cross Opal Creek and bear left on Skyline to the Sea Trail. The route takes you through very tall redwoods, climbs over a ridge (and past a junction with Middle Ridge Road), then returns to the redwoods.

Two miles out you cross the Kelly Creek footbridge, sticking with the Skyline Trail despite the temptations of several side trails. Kelly Creek merges with West Waddell Creek and at 3 miles along travels a course above West Waddell Creek.

Four miles out you'll cross West Waddell Creek on a footbridge. A side trail leads ¹⁄₁₀-mile to a vista point for a closer look at the misty 65-foot falls cascading into the redwood-filled canyon.

Another ½-mile's travel brings you to an overlook of 60-foot Silver Falls and a bit farther Golden Falls, which spill over a reddish gold cliff.

Five miles along, Berry Creek Falls Trail reaches a junction with Sunset Trail, which you'll join, hiking for a time over more open, oak- and madrone-covered slopes before returning to the redwoods.

The path crosses Berry Creek, crests a ridge, and descends to Waddell Creek. Nine and a half miles from the start, you'll cross Middle Ridge Road, descend ½-mile to Dool Trail, travel along redwood-lined Opal Creek, and return to the trailhead via the Opal Creek footbridge.

A trio of waterfalls—your reward for taking this memorable hike.

Big Basin Redwoods State Park

Skyline to the Sea Trail

Terrain: Deep woods, wet world of Waddell and Berry creeks.
Highlights: Redwoods, evergreen forest, even a beach in California's oldest state park.
Distance: 12 miles one way with 1,200-foot elevation loss.
Degree of difficulty: Moderate to strenuous.
Precautions: Slippery trail; bring drinking water.

In 1902 the California state park system was born with the establishment of the California Redwood Park in the Big Basin area of Santa Cruz County. California preserved many more "redwood parks" during the twentieth century, but the redwoods at Big Basin remain one of the gems of the park system.

And one of the gems of the state's trail system—Skyline to the Sea Trail—explores Big Basin Redwoods State Park. As its name suggests, the trail drops from the crest of the Santa Cruz Mountains to the Pacific Ocean.

For the most part, the path runs downhill on its scenic 35-mile journey from Castle Rock State Park to Big Basin Redwoods State Park to Waddell Beach. Views from the Skyline—redwood-forested slopes, fern-smothered canyons, and the great blue Pacific—are superb. The trek from Castle Rock to the sea makes a fine backpacking trip for a three-day weekend.

The wildest and most beautiful part of the Skyline stretches from park headquarters at Big Basin to Waddell Beach and Marsh. It winds through deep woods and explores the moist environments of Waddell and Berry creeks.

Springtime, when the creeks are frothy torrents and Berry Creek Falls cascades at full vigor, is a particularly dramatic season to walk the Skyline to the Sea Trail. During summer, the cool redwood canyons are great places to beat the heat.

Directions to trailhead: From Santa Cruz, drive 12 miles north on Highway 9. Turn west on Highway 236 and proceed 9 miles to Big Basin Redwoods State Park.

If you're hiking from Big Basin to the sea, you'll need to arrange a car shuttle. Waddell Beach, at trail's end, is 18 miles upcoast from Santa Cruz on Highway 1.

Better yet, take the bus, which stops at both the state park and Waddell Beach. One suggestion: leave your car at the Santa Cruz bus station (920 Pacific Avenue) and take the 7:45 A.M. (weekends) bus bound for the state park. You'll arrive about 9:00 A.M.

Hit the trail and take the 5:15 P.M. bus from Waddell Beach back to Santa Cruz. Weekend and weekday schedules differ—and change frequently—so call the Santa Cruz Metropolitan Transit District at (408) 425–8600 for the latest bus schedule.

The walk: The trail begins in the nucleus of the park on Opal Creek flatlands at the bottom of the basin. From park headquarters, join Redwood Trail, which crosses a bridge and travels a few hundred yards to a signed junction with Skyline to the Sea Trail. You'll turn toward the sea and begin a stiff climb out of the basin, passing junctions with other park trails.

After climbing, the trail descends through deep and dark woods, first with Kelly Creek, then along the west fork of Waddell Creek. Ferns and mushrooms, salamanders and banana slugs occupy the wet world of the trail.

Some 4 miles from the trailhead, just short of the confluence of Waddell and Berry creeks, you'll intersect Berry Creek Falls Trail. The falls cascade over fern-covered cliffs into a frothy pool.

An ideal lunch stop or turnaround spot is Sunset Trail Camp, located a mile up Berry Creek Falls Trail and near another falls—Golden Falls.

Skyline to the Sea Trail descends with Waddell Creek and passes through the heart of the beautiful Waddell Valley. Rancho del Oso ("Ranch of the Bear"), as this region is known, has second-generation redwoods, Douglas fir, and Monterey pine, as well as lush meadows.

At 1½ miles from the ocean, you'll reach Twin Redwoods Camp. As you near the sea, the redwoods give way to laurel groves and meadowland. Near trail's end is a freshwater marsh, a favorite stopping place for migratory birds on the Pacific flyway.

A wildlife sanctuary, Theodore J. Hoover Natural Preserve, has been established in the heart of the marsh area for more than 200 kinds of native and migratory birds.

The trail ends at Highway 1. West of the highway is a bus stop and windswept Waddell Beach.

Long Ridge Open Space Preserve

Peters Creek Trail

Terrain: Grassy slopes, hickory oak woodland.
Highlights: Magnificent hickory oaks, grand vistas.
Distance: To Long Ridge is 4 miles round-trip with 400-foot
elevation gain; to Hickory Oak Ridge is 6 miles round-trip.
Degree of difficulty: Moderate.

High on the western slopes of the Santa Cruz Mountains bounding
Skyline Boulevard, Long Ridge Open Space Preserve beckons the
hiker with a hickory oak woodland, grassy slopes, and dramatic
vistas. Twelve miles of trail, including a 3-mile length of the new
Bay Area Ridge Trail, explore the 1,000-acre preserve.

While the premier attraction in most Santa Cruz Mountains parks
is the redwood, here in Long Ridge it's the *Quercus chrolepsi*. With
its 5-foot-diameter trunk and its gargantuan limbs, the hickory oak—
also called canyon oak and gold cup oak—is a sight to behold.

If hiking to the hickory oaks is your sole goal, the easy way to go
is to drive from the main preserve entrance 2 miles south on Skyline Boulevard to a small parking area on the west side of the road.
Follow an old ranch road on a 1½-mile round-trip tour of the hickory oak woodland.

A more ambitious walk begins at the main preserve entrance,
tours Peters Creek, then climbs Long Ridge. From the ridge top,
you can extend your walk to the hickory oaks.

Directions to trailhead: From Skyline Boulevard, at Saratoga
Gap, drive north 3 miles to a parking area on the west side of the
road.

The walk: The path leads over grassy slopes into a woodland and
crosses Peters Creek. Note the trail leading north (Peters Creek
Loop Trail), but pass it by for now and continue upcreek through a
narrow canyon overhung with oak and fir.

Leaving the canyon, you'll turn uphill, joining an old road climbing Long Ridge to a trail junction. You save another branch of the
Peters Creek Loop Trail for your return trip and turn left to reach
the ridge top.

Enjoy the view of Big Basin Redwoods State Park as well as
many more timbered ridges and hollows and the deep-blue Pacific.

Hickory oak–bound hikers will continue along the west side of the ridge, crossing grassy slopes and descending to the woodlands of the Hickory Oak Ridge Area.

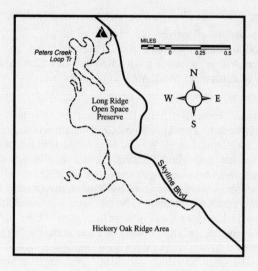

Henry Cowell Redwoods State Park

River, Eagle Creek, Pine, Ridge Trails

Terrain: Redwood groves, oak woodland.
Highlights: Grand redwoods, coastal views.
Distance: 4 miles round-trip with 500-foot elevation gain.
Degree of difficulty: Moderate.

Henry Cowell Redwoods State Park preserves first- and second-growth redwoods in a tranquil Santa Cruz Mountains setting.

Henry Cowell and Joseph Welch, who in the 1860s acquired the former Mexican land grant Rancho Cañada de Rincón, shared a commitment to protect the Big Trees Grove (now Redwood Grove). Welch's holdings were purchased by Santa Cruz County in 1930 and became parkland; in the 1950s this land was combined with 1,500 acres donated by Cowell's heirs to become a state park.

Thanks to the preservation efforts of these men, the "Big Trees" are as stirring a sight now as they were a century ago when railroad passengers between San Jose and Santa Cruz made a lunch stop among the tall trees.

The short Redwood Grove Nature Trail, which visits one of the finest first-growth groves south of San Francisco, is a good place to start your exploration of the Santa Cruz Mountains. This popular trail, complete with interpretive leaflet, loops along the San Lorenzo riverbank among the redwoods, some of which have been given names. One of the larger commemorative redwoods honors President Theodore Roosevelt, who visited the grove in 1903.

The state park is hilly, and with changes in elevation come changes in vegetation. Moisture-loving redwoods predominate on the lowlands while the park's upper ridges are cloaked with oak woodland and chaparral.

By connecting four of the park's trails, you can walk through all the park's diverse ecosystems. You'll begin in the redwoods and ascend chaparral-covered slopes to an observation deck located in the middle of the park. Great mountain and coastal views reward your ascent.

Be sure to stop at the nature center, which has exhibits and sells maps and books. Redwood Grove Nature Trail begins near the center.

Directions to trailhead: Henry Cowell Redwoods State Park is located just south of Felton on Highway 9. You can pick up River Trail near the park entrance at Highway 9 or from the picnic area.

The walk: River Trail meanders downriver along the east bank of the San Lorenzo. You may hear the whistle of the Roaring Camp and Big Trees Railroad, a popular tourist attraction located next to the park. The steam-powered train takes passengers through the Santa Cruz Mountains on a narrow-gauge track.

About ¼-mile after River Trail passes beneath a Southern Pacific railroad trestle, you'll intersect Eagle Creek Trail and begin ascending out of the redwood forest along Eagle Creek. Madrone and manzanita predominate on the exposed sunny slopes.

Bear right on Pine Trail (the pines you'll see en route are ponderosa pine) and climb steeply to the observation deck. Enjoy the view of the Monterey and Santa Cruz coastline, the redwood forests, and that tumbled-up range of mountains called Santa Cruz.

On the return trip, take Ridge Trail on a steep descent to River Trail. Both River Trail and its nearly parallel path, Pipeline Road, lead back to Redwood Grove and the picnic area.

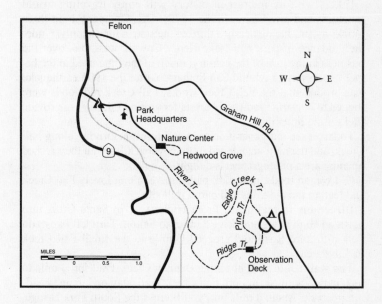

Fall Creek

Bennett Creek, North Fork, South Fork Trails

> **Terrain:** Forks of Fall Creek, redwood and Douglas fir forests.
> **Highlights:** Lush creek environment, historic limekilns.
> **Distance:** Loop to limekilns is 3½ miles round-trip; to mill site is 6¾ miles round-trip.
> **Degree of difficulty:** Moderate.

The forks of Fall Creek and a forest of second-generation redwoods and Douglas fir are some of the attractions of a walk through this isolated area of Henry Cowell Redwoods State Park. Located on the slopes of Ben Lomond Mountain in a wild canyon northwest of Felton, this part of the park also boasts a lush creekside habitat of ferns, big-leaf maple, and alder.

Hikers with an interest in history will enjoy traveling to old limekilns and a mill site. In the 1870s, IXL Company built three limekilns, producing nearly a third of the state's lime supply. Under the guidance of park namesake Henry Cowell, who took over the business at the turn of the century, much of the lime used in the cement necessary to rebuild San Francisco after the 1906 earthquake was produced at the Fall Creek works. Fall Creek redwoods were logged to construct redwood barrels for storing lime and to provide fuel for the limekilns.

Today, a second-generation redwood forest is thriving along Fall Creek, and the long-abandoned moss-covered kilns with their arched opening are a photographer's delight.

Old wagon roads, now park paths, travel along lovely Fall Creek and lead to the old kilns and barrel mill site.

Directions to trailhead: From Highway 1 in Santa Cruz, turn north on Highway 9 and drive 5 miles to Felton. Turn left (west) on Felton-Empire Road and proceed ½-mile to the small Fall Creek parking area.

The walk: Join switchbacking Bennett Creek Trail for ¼-mile to its junction with North Fork Fall Creek Trail, staying left and heading upcreek. About a mile out, you'll cross the South Fork Bridge, pass an intersection with South Fork Trail (your return route), and continue along the North Fork of Fall Creek through a mixed woodland of redwood, fir, tan oak, and maple.

Another ½-mile walk brings you to Cape Horn Trail junction. Those inclined toward a shorter (3½-mile) Fall Creek exploration should go left here.

North Fork hikers cross the creek on twin logs and enter redwood forest. Regard the ruins of Barrel Mill and continue through the redwoods to trail's end at a tiny dam 3¼ miles from the trailhead.

Retrace your steps to Cape Horn Trail, a dirt road that soon leaves the creek, climbs a short while, then descends to the South Fork of Fall Creek and the limekiln area. Next you'll join South Fork Trail and follow it ½-mile back to North Fork Trail, turning right and walking a mile back to the trailhead.

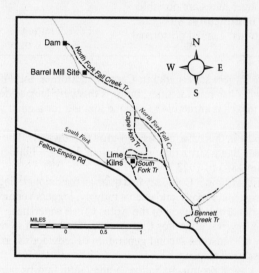

Forest of Nisene Marks State Park

Loma Prieta Grade Trail

> **Terrain:** Maze of ridges and canyons filled with second-growth redwood forest and oak woodlands.
> **Highlights:** A rugged, little-developed park with 30 miles of hiking trails.
> **Distance:** From Porter Picnic Area to Hoffman's Historic Site is 6 miles round-trip with 400-foot elevation gain. Several longer hikes are possible.
> **Degree of difficulty:** Moderate.
> **Precautions:** Lots of poison oak.

One of the largest state parks in Central California, the Forest of Nisene Marks has few facilities, but it is this very lack of development that makes it attractive to anyone looking for a quiet walk in the woods.

The woods, in this case, are second-growth redwoods. The park is on land near Santa Cruz that was clear-cut during a lumber boom lasting from 1883 to 1923.

Loma Prieta Lumber Company had quite an operation. Using steam engines, oxen, skid roads, and even a railway, loggers ventured into nearly every narrow canyon of the Aptos Creek watershed.

After the loggers left Aptos Canyon, the forest began to regenerate. Today a handsome second generation of redwoods is rising to cover the scarred slopes.

The Markses, a prominent Salinas Valley farm family, purchased the land in the 1950s. In 1963 the three Marks children donated the property to the state in the name of their mother, Nisene Marks. As specified in the deed, the forest must not be developed and the natural process of regeneration must be allowed to continue.

Ferocious winter storms in 1982 and 1983 battered the canyons and ruined part of the park's trail system, in particular the paths in the upper reaches of Aptos Canyon. Railroad grades and trestles that had withstood a century of storms were washed away. Volunteers and the California Conservation Corps repaired the damage.

Loma Prieta Grade Trail follows parts of an old railway bed. A narrow-gauge steam railway ran from a mill to China Camp. A few ramshackle wooden buildings are all that remain of this turn-of-the-century lumber camp that once housed three hundred workers.

Directions to trailhead: From Highway 1 in Aptos, take the Aptos/Seacliff exit to Soquel Drive. Turn right (east) and proceed a ½-mile into Aptos. Turn left on Aptos Creek Road and drive 4 miles to a locked gate at the Forest of Nisene Marks's Porter Picnic Area.

The walk: From the picnic area, follow Aptos Creek ⅖-mile to the Loma Prieta Grade trailhead. (An old mill site is a short walk up the road.)

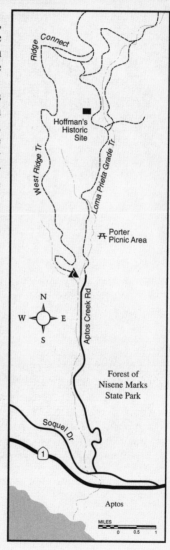

For a short stretch, the trail stays near Aptos Creek. This creek, which rises high on Santa Rosalia Ridge, is joined by the waters of Bridge Creek, then spills into Monterey Bay at Rio Del Mar Beach. Silver salmon and steelhead spawn in the creek.

The abandoned railway bed makes a gentle trail except for a few places where the old bridges have collapsed into steep ravines. Your destination of China Camp, now called Hoffman's Historic Site, has a few wooden structures.

You can return the same way or take the Ridge Connect Trail over to West Ridge Trail. This latter trail runs south and connects with Aptos Creek Road near the trailhead. Be warned that you may have to share Ridge Trail with large amounts of poison oak.

Thanks to conservationists, a first generation and second generation of redwoods are protected from logging.

2. San Mateo/Santa Cruz County Coasts

North of Monterey Bay and south of San Francisco Bay are the coastlines of San Mateo and Santa Cruz counties. Bold headlands and miles of sandy beach characterize this coast, parts of which have been popular with tourists for more than a century.

Two wildlife dramas along this coast attract visitors from around the world. At Año Nuevo State Reserve, walkers on guided tours get close-up looks at a large population of elephant seals. And during autumn, the eucalyptus grove at Natural Bridges State Beach hosts the largest gathering of monarch butterflies in America.

Families tend to love a day at the beach in Santa Cruz. The town's earthquake-prompted rebuilding efforts have not overwhelmed its funkiness and laid-backedness. The mellow mile-long beach is most relaxing, cruising the boardwalk is fun for kids of all ages, and riding the world-famous Giant Dipper Roller Coaster is like totally awesome.

And for the family that likes to hike, there are a couple of close-by natural attractions: the inspiring redwoods of Pogonip Park next to the UC Santa Cruz campus and the ranch buildings and backcountry of Wilder Ranch State Historic Park.

San Mateo County highlights include a hike up Montara Mountain for a view from Half Moon Bay to the Golden Gate; a visit to Fitzgerald Marine Reserve, one of the best tide-pool areas on the Central Coast; and a mellow walk along the low sandy hills by Half Moon Bay.

McNee Ranch State Park

Montara Mountain Trail

> **Terrain:** Coastal scrub–covered Montara Mountain, far
> northern extension of Santa Cruz Mountains.
> **Highlights:** Fabulous coastal vistas from Half Moon Bay to
> the Golden Gate.
> **Distance:** 7½ miles round-trip with 2,000-foot elevation gain.
> **Degree of difficulty:** Moderate to strenuous.

Not even a sign welcomes you to McNee Ranch State Park, located
on the San Mateo County coast 25 miles south of San Francisco.
But what the park lacks in signs and facilities, it makes up in grand
views and wide-open spaces. And oh, what a view! The coastline
from Half Moon Bay to the Golden Gate National Recreation Area
is at your feet.

The panoramic view is a hiker's reward for the rigorous ascent of
Montara Mountain, whose slopes make up the bulk of the state
park. Montara Mountain, geologists say, is a 90-million-year-old
chunk of granite (largely quartz diorite) that forms the northernmost extension of the Santa Cruz Mountains.

Alas, what is a beautiful park to hikers is an ideal location for a
multilane highway to the California Department of Transportation.
Caltrans wants to build a Highway 1 bypass through the park to re-
place the existing landslide-prone stretch of highway known as the
Devil's Slide that begins about 2 miles south of Pacifica.

Caltrans and its building plans have been fiercely contested by
environmentalists, who fear the highway bypass would completely
destroy the ambiance of the park and lead to further development in
the area. The two sides have been battling it out in court for several
years.

At the moment, it's not cement but the coastal scrub community—
ceanothus, sage, and monkey flower—that predominates on the
mountain. The park also boasts several flower-strewn grasslands.
Meandering down Montara Mountain is willow- and alder-lined
Martini Creek, which forms the southern boundary of the state park.

The park's trail system includes footpaths as well as Old San Pedro
Road, a dirt track that's popular with mountain bikers. Little hiker
symbols keep walkers on the trail, but since all routes climb Mon-

tara Mountain and more or less meet at the top, don't be overly concerned about staying on the "right" trail.

Opposite the state park, across Coast Highway, is Montara State Beach. This ½-mile sand strand is a popular surfing, fishing, and picnicking spot.

Hikers will note that the nearest place for provisions is the hamlet of Montara, where there's a café and grocery store. Good accommodations for hikers on a budget may be found at the Montara Lighthouse Hostel right on the coast. The 30-bed hostel, situated next to a working lighthouse, has kitchen facilities, a volleyball court, and even an outdoor hot tub.

Directions to trailhead: Take Highway 1 to Montara and park in the fair-sized lot at the north end of Montara State Beach. Walk carefully 150 yards upcoast and cross the highway. The unsigned trail begins at a pipe gate across a fire road on the inland side of Coast Highway.

The walk: Head up the fire road a short distance and join the trail on your left. The path swings north (upcoast) over a seasonally flowered grassy slope, drops to join a dirt road, then begins ascending once more.

As you climb, you pass two benches, strategically placed for you to catch your breath. The dirt road eventually swings south, but you join a footpath and ascend to a saddle. Two trails lead left to the peak and terrific views.

Below you, upcoast, is the town of Pacifica and beyond that, the Golden Gate Bridge and San Francisco Bay. To the east is Mount Diablo. Way out to sea on the far horizon are the Farallon Islands.

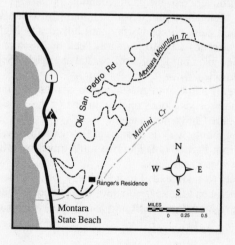

43

San Pedro Valley County Park

Brooks Falls Overlook Trail

> **Terrain:** Valley tucked in northern Santa Cruz Mountains.
> **Highlights:** Impressive Brooks Falls.
> **Distance:** 1½ miles round-trip.
> **Degree of difficulty:** Easy.

Tucked in the far-northern Santa Cruz Mountains near Pacifica, San Pedro Valley Park offers walkers a variety of streamside strolls and hillside hikes. Hikers will note that San Pedro Valley is often sunny when more coastal locales nearby are fog-bound.

Flowing through the valley are the south and middle forks of San Pedro Creek, watercourses that attract spawning steelhead during winter months. Beautiful Brooks Falls, a 175-foot, three-tiered cascade, is the park's most notable attraction.

During California's mission era, San Pedro Valley was under cultivation by workers from San Francisco's Mission Dolores who grew wheat, fruits, and vegetables. In this century, pumpkins and artichokes have been the commercial crops of choice.

For a glimpse into local history, as well as a quick study of the valley's flora and wildlife, stop in at the park visitor center. Short, self-guided Plaskon Nature Trail, behind the visitor center, provides an introduction to the plants found in the park.

Montara Mountain Trail, a 5-mile round-trip with a stiff 1,400-foot elevation gain, climbs brushy park hillsides to McNee Ranch Trail, then ascends onward to North Peak of Montara Mountain. This is a nice hike, but I prefer the coastal approach. (See the Montara Mountain walk.)

Another stiff climb with coastal views is a loop on the Hazelnut Trail, which ascends slopes thick with one of the park's predominant plants, the California hazelnut.

A mellow family walk is a loop via Brooks Falls Overlook Trail and Old Trout Farm Trail. The two trails travel by a frisky creek and offer a vista of the falls.

Directions to trailhead: From Highway 1 in Pacifica, drive 1⅕ miles southeast on Linda Mar Boulevard to its end at Oddstad Boulevard. Turn right, then turn left into San Pedro Valley County Park.

Brooks Falls Overlook Trail begins at the rear of the parking lot by the restrooms.

The walk: Begin a mild ascent, continuing through a nonindigenous woodland of eucalyptus and Monterey pine. A ½-mile along, take a seat on a bench that overlooks bubbling Brooks Creek and Brooks Falls.

From the overlook, the trail winds another ½-mile down to a junction with Old Trout Farm Trail, a dirt road that returns you to the trailhead in ½-mile.

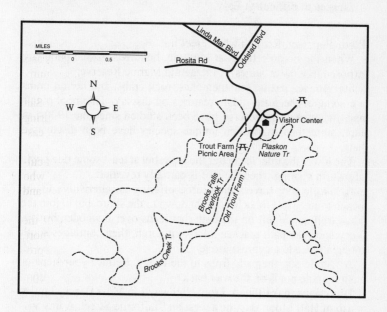

Fitzgerald Marine Reserve

Reserve Trail

Terrain: Shallow reef.
Highlights: Excellent tide-pooling.
Distance: 1 mile round-trip.
Degree of difficulty: Easy.

Plop, plop, fizz, fizz. Oh what a reef it is.

When the ocean retreats at low tide, hundreds of tide pools are exposed to view at James V. Fitzgerald Marine Reserve.

Starfish, sea snails, sea anemones, rock crabs, and hermit crabs are some of the many tidal creatures on display. Tide-pool plants and creatures at the reserve have been studied since the 1920s; in fact, more than two dozen unique species have been discovered here.

The lower the tide, the better the look, but at least some tide pools are worth visiting when the reef is partially revealed.

A ½-mile trail travels the bluffs, offering an alternative to the beach route. Most folks head right down to the shore, but to join the bluff trail, angle left on the path that leads over a wooden bridge. Very soon the path reaches a lookout perch, then continues south along a fence to a cypress grove.

A ½-mile out, the path drops to the beach. Retrace your steps or visit the tide pools on the way back.

Directions to trailhead: From Highway 1 in Moss Beach, 7 miles north of Half Moon Bay, turn west on California Street. A tiny visitor center is located at the edge of the parking lot.

Half Moon Bay

Coastside Trail

> **Terrain:** Bay-side beach, low dunes.
> **Highlights:** Mellow walk along the bay.
> **Distance:** From Francis Beach to Roosevelt Beach is 6 miles round-trip.
> **Degree of difficulty:** Easy.

From East Breakwater, Half Moon Bay arcs southward, backed by a long sandy beach. Backdropping the beach are eroded cliffs and low dunes.

Three miles of shoreline and four beaches—Roosevelt, Dunes, Venice, and Francis—make up Half Moon Bay State Park. Extending north of the park is more accessible—and walkable—shoreline.

Coastside Trail, along the park's eastern boundary, is a multiuse pathway open to cyclists and walkers. Depending on the tide, you can return via the beach. Coastside Trail is a better bike ride than walk; its function is to link the various state beaches and it does that quite well, but it isn't all that interesting a saunter. It does, however, bring some marvelous beaches within reach, and for that reason is worth the walk.

Directions to trailhead: From Highway 1 in the town of Half Moon Bay (¼-mile north of the intersection with Highway 92), turn west on Kelly Avenue and drive to Francis Beach. There is a state park day-use fee.

The walk: The trail winds past low sandy hills, dotted by clumps of cordgrass. At trail's end you can extend your walk by beach-combing northward toward Pillar Harbor by way of Miramar Beach and El Granada Beach.

Pescadero Marsh

Sequoia Audubon Trail

Terrain: Lagoon and estuary.
Highlights: Great bird-watching.
Distance: From Pescadero State Beach to North Marsh is 2½ miles round-trip; to North Pond is also 2½ miles round-trip.
Degree of difficulty: Easy.
Precautions: The North Pond area is closed between March 15 and September 1.

Bring a pair of binoculars to Pescadero Marsh Natural Preserve, the largest marsh between Monterey Bay and San Francisco. Pescadero Creek and Butano Creek pool resources to form a lagoon and estuary that is a haven for birds, and a heaven for bird-watchers.

Peer through willows, tules, and cattails, and you might spot diving ducks, great egrets, or yellow-throated warblers. More than 180 species of birds have been sighted in the preserve.

The best bird-watching is in late fall and early spring. To protect the birds during their breeding season, the northernmost preserve trail is closed part of the year.

You may take one of the walks described below, or simply wander the perimeter of the marsh to one of the wooden observation decks and begin your bird-watching.

Directions to trailhead: Pescadero State Beach and Pescadero Marsh Natural Preserve are located off Highway 1, some 15 miles south of Half Moon Bay. The state beach has three parking areas. The largest is at the south end of the beach, where Pescadero Road forms a junction with Highway 1.

The walk: From the southernmost beach parking area, follow the beach north. If it's low tide, you'll get a good look at some fascinating tide pools.

A ½-mile's walk brings you to the mouth of Butano Creek. You may have to hike inland a bit to find a place to ford the creek.

Turn inland and pass under the highway bridge. You'll join Sequoia Audubon Trail, which meanders between the south shore of North Marsh and the north bank of Butano Creek. Take the first fork to the left and loop toward North Marsh. A right turn, as you near the marsh, will allow you to loop back to the Sequoia Audubon Trail.

To North Pond: Walk north on Pescadero Beach. A ½-mile beyond Butano Creek, you'll come to the massive cliff faces of San Mateo Coast State Beaches. (With a low tide, you could walk along the base of the cliffs to San Gregorio Beach.) Turn inland to the northern Pescadero State Beach parking area. Directly across the road from the entrance to the parking lot is the trailhead for North Marsh Trail.

Follow the ½-mile path as it loops around North Pond. Cattle graze the slopes above the pond, and abundant bird life populates the surrounding thickets. The path climbs a small hill where a wooden observation deck affords a grand view of the large North Marsh.

You can return by taking the trail south and to the left. It leads to Sequoia Audubon Trail, which in turn takes you under the Butano Creek Bridge. You then follow the beach back to your starting point.

West Butano Loop: For another fine bird walk, transport yourself ½-mile up Pescadero Road. Entry to the small, dirt parking area is almost directly opposite the San Mateo County road maintenance station.

The unsigned trail leads north from the parking area and winds through a wide, lush meadow. When you get to the creek, follow the trail east (rightward). As you follow Butano Creek, you'll be walking the tops of dikes that once allowed coastal farmers to use this rich bottomland for growing artichokes, Brussels sprouts, and beans. Adjacent lands are still carefully cultivated by local farmers.

Watch for blue herons and snowy egrets. Perhaps you'll even spot the San Francisco garter snake, an endangered species. After following Butano Creek through the marsh, you'll join the trail to the right to return to the starting point.

Bean Hollow State Beach

Arroyo de los Frijoles Trail

Terrain: Pebbled beach.
Highlights: Tide pools, shoreline of polished stones.
Distance: From Pebble Beach to Bean Hollow Beach is 2
   miles round-trip.
Degree of difficulty: Easy.

Pebble Beach—not to be confused with the Pebble Beach of eigh-
teen-hole renown near Carmel, the Pebble Beach in Tomales Bay
State Park, or the Pebble Beach near Crescent City—is one of those
enchanting San Mateo County beaches that extend from Año Nuevo
State Reserve to Thornton State Beach, a bit south of San Francisco.
The pebbles on the beach are quartz chipped from an offshore reef,
tumbled ashore, then wave-polished and rounded into beautifully
hued small stones.

The 1-mile walk between Pebble Beach and Bean Hollow Beach
offers a close-up look at tide pools, wildflowers (in season), and
colonies of harbor seals and shorebirds.

Some walkers say that the San Mateo County beaches and bluffs
remind them of the British coast near Cornwall. This comparison is
reinforced at the beginning of the trail, which crosses a moorlike
environment bedecked with irises and daisies.

The rocky intertidal area is habitat for sea slugs and snails,
anemones, and urchins. Bird-watchers will sight cormorants, pelicans, and red-billed oystercatchers flying over the water. The sandy
beach is patrolled by gulls, sandpipers, and sanderlings.

Directions to trailhead: Pebble Beach is located 40 miles south
of San Francisco. The beach is off Highway 1, about 2½ miles south
of Pescadero. The trail begins at the south end of the parking lot.

The walk: The first part of the walk is along a nature trail. Waves
crashing over the offshore reef are a dramatic sight. Keep an eye
out for harbor seals swimming just offshore.

A couple of small footbridges aid your crossing of rivulets that
carve the coastal bluffs. To the south, you'll get a glimpse of Pigeon Point Lighthouse, now part of a hostel. If the tide is low when
you approach Bean Hollow State Beach, head down to the sand.

Arroyo de los Frijoles ("Creek of the Beans") empties into Lake Lucerne, just east of Pacific Coast Highway. The state beach originally had the Spanish name before being Americanized to Bean Hollow. Picnic tables at the beach suggest a lunch or rest stop.

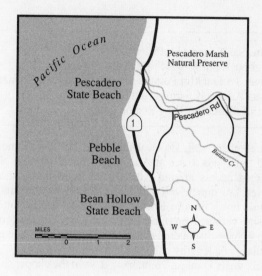

51

Cascade Creek/Northern Año Nuevo State Reserve

Cascade Creek, Año Nuevo Bluff Trails

> **Terrain:** Sand dunes, bluffs, rock coves.
> **Highlights:** Wildlife-watching, isolated beaches.
> **Distance:** To Franklin Point is 3 miles round-trip; to Gazos Coastal Access is 5 miles round-trip.
> **Degree of difficulty:** Easy to moderate.

True, the elephant seals do steal the show, but there's more than bellowing pinnipeds to see at Año Nuevo State Reserve. North of the restricted access around Año Nuevo Point is a coastline of rocky coves, low dunes, and wildflower-strewn meadowlands.

The dunes north of Año Nuevo Point are colorfully dotted with yellow sand verbena, morning glory, and beach strawberry. Archaeologists have discovered evidence—chipped tools and mounds of seashells—of a lengthy occupation by native peoples.

This walk visits Franklin Point, named when the clipper ship *John Franklin* rammed into the rocks here in 1865. At low tide, the

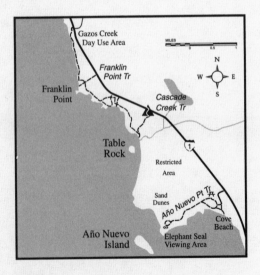

point's tide pools can be visited. Seals and sea otters may often be glimpsed from Franklin Point.

The walk can be extended by traveling the bluff trail north to Gazos Creek Coastal Access, a favorite of the surf-fishing set; however, this path is irregularly maintained and often crowded with poison oak.

Directions to trailhead: From Highway 1, proceed 2⅕ miles north of the main Año Nuevo State Reserve entrance to a turnout on the west side of the road.

The walk: Follow the dirt road a short ½-mile west across grassy bluffs to a small cypress and eucalyptus grove. Head north over low bluffs, perhaps detouring to visit the wild beach just below. A mile out, a right-forking path leads to Highway 1, but you take the left fork and descend toward a cove at the mouth of Whitehouse Creek.

You'll cross the creek and continue hiking north along the bluffs to Franklin Point. Watch the marine mammals, retrace your steps, or head north on a more tentative, poison oak–compromised trail.

Año Nuevo State Reserve

Año Nuevo Trail

> **Terrain:** Sand dunes.
> **Highlights:** Huge population of elephant seals, guided walks.
> **Distance:** 3 miles round-trip.
> **Degree of difficulty:** Easy to moderate.

One of the best New Year's resolutions a walker could make is to plan a winter trip to Año Nuevo State Reserve. Here you'll be treated to a wildlife drama that attracts visitors from all over the world—a close-up look at the largest mainland population of elephant seals.

From December through April, a colony of the huge creatures visits Año Nuevo Island and Point to breed and bear young. To protect the elephant seals (and the humans who hike out to see them), the reserve is open only through naturalist-guided tours during these months.

Slaughtered for their oil-rich blubber, elephant seals numbered fewer than 100 by the turn of the century but rebounded rapidly when placed under government protection. Año Nuevo State Reserve was created in 1958 to protect the huge mammals.

Male elephant seals, some reaching lengths of 16 feet and weighing 3 tons, arrive in December and begin battling for dominance. Only a very small percentage of males get to inseminate a female; most remain lifelong bachelors. The females, relatively svelte at 1,200 to 2,000 pounds, come ashore in January and join the harems of the dominant males.

La Punta del Año Nuevo ("The Point of the New Year") was named by the Spanish explorer Sebastián Vizcaino on January 3, 1603. It's one of the oldest place-names in California.

At the time of its discovery by Europeans, the point was occupied by the Ohlone, who lived off the bounty of the sea. Judging from kitchen midden sites—shell mounds—found in the nearby dunes, it was a rich bounty indeed.

The Año Nuevo area later hosted a variety of enterprises. From the 1850s to 1920, redwood cut from the slopes of the nearby Santa Cruz Mountains was shipped from Año Nuevo Bay. A dairy industry flourished on the coastal bluffs. The reserve's visitor center is a restored century-old dairy barn.

While the elephant seals are clearly the main attraction when they come ashore during the winter to breed and during the spring and summer to molt, the reserve is still fascinating even when the big creatures are not in residence; in fact, Año Nuevo is a year-round destination.

Bird-watchers may glimpse a cliff swallow, Western gull, red-tailed hawk, and many other inland and shorebirds.

The beautiful sand dunes of the reserve are covered with beach grass, morning glory, and extensive patches of beach strawberry.

Joining the elephant seals on Año Nuevo Island are Steller sea lions, California sea lions, and harbor seals. Seals inhabit Año Nuevo year-round. Viewing is great in the spring and summer months—on the beaches. Autumn brings one- to three-year-old "yearling" seals ashore to rest on the beaches.

Reservations and information: Año Nuevo Point, where the elephant seals reside, is open only to visitors on guided walks. State park volunteer naturalists conduct these 2½-hour, 3-mile walks daily from December through March.

Advance reservations for the guided walks are strongly recommended. Reservations may be made through MISTIX, the state park system's reservation contractor, by calling 1–800–444–PARK. Credit card payment is accepted.

From April through November, access to the Año Nuevo Point Wildlife Protection Area is by permit only. Permits are issued free of charge daily at the reserve, on a first-come, first-served basis.

Directions to trailhead: Año Nuevo State Reserve is located just west of Highway 1, 22 miles north of Santa Cruz and 30 miles south of Half Moon Bay.

The ungainly elephant seal is the main attraction at Año Nuevo, but there's plenty to enjoy even when they're gone.

Wilder Ranch State Historic Park
Old Landing Cove, Ohlone Bluff Trails

Terrain: Coastal bluffs, both wild and cultivated.
Highlights: Historic dairy ranch, dramatic bluffs, more
  Brussels sprouts than you've ever seen in your life.
Distance: 2 miles round-trip; to Four Mile Beach is 10½
  miles round-trip.
Degree of difficulty: Easy to moderate.

At Wilder Ranch State Historic Park, located on the coast just north of Santa Cruz, you get the feeling that not one stone has gone unpreserved. The Brussels sprouts fields are in an agricultural preserve, the former Wilder Ranch is in a cultural preserve, and Wilder Beach is now a natural preserve for the benefit of nesting snowy plovers. All these preserves are found within Wilder Ranch State Historic Park, which in turn preserves some 4,000 acres of beach, bluffs, and inland canyons.

Rancho del Matadero was started here by Mission Santa Cruz in 1791. The Wilder family operated what was by all accounts a very successful and innovative dairy for nearly 100 years. The California Department of Parks and Recreation acquired the land in 1974.

The Wilders' ranch buildings, barn, gardens, and Victorian house still stand, and are open to public tours. The parks department is slowly restoring the area to reflect its historical use as a dairy.

In addition to the guided historic walks, the park boasts Old Landing Cove Trail, a bluff-top path that, as its name suggests, leads to a historic cove. From the 1850s to the 1890s, schooners dropped anchor in this cove to load lumber. Observant hikers will spot iron rings, which supported landing chutes, still embedded in the cliffs.

Brussels sprouts fans will see more of this vegetable than they ever dreamed possible; fully 12 percent of the nation's production is grown in the state park.

Directions to trailhead: From Santa Cruz, head north on Coast Highway 4 miles to the signed turnoff for Wilder Ranch State Historic Park on the ocean side of the highway. Follow the park road to its end at a large parking lot, where the signed trail begins.

The walk: The path, an old ranch road, heads coastward. Signs warn you not to turn left toward Wilder Beach, where the snowy plovers dwell, and discourage you from heading right, where pesticides are used on the fields of Brussels sprouts.

The trail offers a bird's-eye view of the surf surging into a sea cave, then turns north and follows the cliff edge.

Old Landing Cove is small—so small that you wonder how the coastal schooners of old managed to maneuver into its confines. If it's low tide, you might see harbor seals resting atop the flat rocks offshore. Another natural attraction at the cove is a fern-filled sea cave. The ferns are watered by an underground spring.

The trail continues another ½-mile along the bluffs to a sandy beach. This is a good turnaround point (for a 3½-mile round-trip).

Ambitious hikers will continue north another 3½ miles along land's end, following footpaths and ranch roads past Strawberry Beach and Three Mile Beach, retreating inland now and then to bypass deep gullies, and finally arriving at the park's north boundary at Four Mile Beach. A splendid coastal hike!

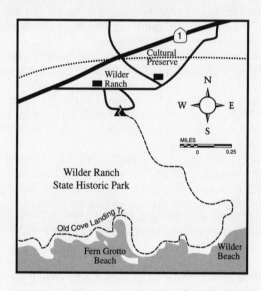

Wilder Ranch State Historic Park

Wilder Ridge Loop Trail

Terrain: Grassy uplands, wooded canyons.
Highlights: Monterey Bay vistas.
Distance: From Cultural Preserve to Wilder Ridge Overlook
  is 6½ miles round-trip with 500-foot elevation gain.
Degree of difficulty: Moderate.

Wilder Ranch is much more than a historic ranch; the 3,900-acre park boasts grassy ridges, woodlands, and second-generation redwood groves.

Some 35 miles of trails crisscross the park uplands. Walkers should note that this is prime mountain bike terrain and that cyclists are permitted on all roads and trails. Mountain bikers outnumber hikers by a significant margin in this park.

One good introduction to the park's inland reaches is the climb to Wilder Ridge. Fine Monterey Bay views are the hiker's reward for the ascent.

Directions to trailhead: From Santa Cruz, drive north on Coast Highway 4 miles to the signed turnoff for Wilder Ranch State Historic Park on the ocean side of the highway. Follow the park road to its end at a large parking lot.

The walk: From the parking area, walk the paved road through the historic ranch, continuing on a gravel road and reaching the Highway 1 underpass in ¼-mile. Proceed to a big bulletin board, then a few more paces to a signed junction with Wilder Ridge Loop Trail, an old ranch road on the left.

After a mile's mellow ascent, the path splits and you can begin a counterclockwise climb to the top of Wilder Ridge. Once you've taken in the coastal vistas from the overlook, you can shorten your return via the Zane Gray Cutoff, lengthen it by joining several other park paths, or continue your circuit on Wilder Ridge Loop Trail.

Natural Bridges State Beach

Monarch Trail

> **Terrain:** Beach, lagoon, eucalyptus grove.
> **Highlights:** Largest concentration of monarch butterflies, superb tide-pool exploration.
> **Distance:** ¾-mile round-trip.
> **Degree of difficulty:** Easy.

Until October 1989 when the devastating Loma Prieta earthquake shook Santa Cruz, it was easy to see why the beach here was named Natural Bridges. Alas, this strong temblor doomed the last remaining natural bridge.

While its offshore bridges are but a memory, this park on the outskirts of Santa Cruz nevertheless offers plenty of natural attractions. A eucalyptus grove in the center of the park hosts the largest concentration of monarch butterflies in America. The park has an extensive interpretive program from October through March, when the monarchs winter at the grove. Another park highlight is a superb rocky tide-pool area, habitat for mussels, limpets, barnacles, and sea urchins.

The natural bridges have crumbled into memory, but the name remains.

After you explore the park, visit nearby Long Marine Laboratory, located just upcoast at the end of Delaware Avenue. UC Santa Cruz faculty and students use the research facility, which studies coastal ecology. The lab's Marine Aquarium is open to the public by docent tours from 1:00 to 4:00 P.M., Tuesday through Sunday.

Directions to trailhead: Natural Bridges State Beach is located off Highway 1 in Santa Cruz at 2531 West Cliff Drive. Follow the signs from Highway 1.

The walk: Signed Monarch Trail begins near the park's small interpretive center. Soon the trail splits; the leftward fork leads to a monarch observation platform. Sometimes on cold mornings, the butterflies look like small, brown, fluttering leaves. As the sun warms the insects, the "leaves" come to life, bobbing and darting. In spring and summer the monarchs—easily the country's most recognized butterfly—leave their coastal California birthplace and disperse across America. Winters, however, are spent on the frost-free California coast—from Santa Cruz to Southern California to northern Baja. As many as 200,000 monarchs cluster in the state park in a "good" butterfly year.

The other branch of the trail is a self-guided nature walk. It ends in a grove of Monterey pine.

When you head back to the visitor center, detour down to the beach. Just up the beach is Secret Lagoon, the domain of ducks and great blue herons. Farther up the beach is one of the Central Coast's truly superb tide-pool areas.

▲
Pogonip

Old Stables, Brayshaw, Spring Trails

Terrain: Redwood groves, mixed evergreen forest, meadows.

Highlights: Superb backdrop to UC Santa Cruz; views of Monterey Bay and San Lorenzo Valley.

Distance: 4 miles round-trip with 200-foot elevation gain.

Degree of difficulty: Moderate.

Few universities can boast the scenic surroundings of the University of California at Santa Cruz. Set amid stands of redwood and mountain meadows, the campus commands a grand view of Monterey Bay.

One way to visit the university is to walk the campus itself, which is divided into eight colleges, each constructed in a different architectural style. Another way to go is to hike the Pogonip, a wild city park next to the campus. Pogonip, a 600-acre preserve of shady glens and sunny meadows, is a walker's delight.

Henry Cowell, who left his mark on Santa Cruz in so many ways, owned a limestone quarry and lime-making operation during the last decades of the previous century and into this century as well. In 1961 the state of California purchased a 2,000-acre parcel of the old Cowell Ranch as the site for UC Santa Cruz. The area that is now Pogonip Park was acquired from Cowell's heirs in 1989.

The native Ohlone, acute observers of the natural world, called this land Pogonip, meaning "icy fog." Fog, both chilly and tepid, often enshrouds Pogonip's evergreen forest (oak, madrone, bay) and second-growth redwood groves. One frequently seen denizen of the wet forest floor is the banana slug, the popular mascot of UC Santa Cruz.

A network of trails and service roads crosses Pogonip, a City of Santa Cruz park. The trails are mostly unsigned, so first-time visitors need to know where they're going. Some trails on the park map such as Pogonip Creek (overgrown, no footbridges) and Haunted Meadow (incomplete) are inviting, but difficult for a newcomer to the area to negotiate.

Two favorite loops explore the south and north areas of the park. My favorite southern loop (about 3½ miles) is Brayshaw Trail to

Spring Trail to Lookout Trail to Pogonip Creek Trail. Redwoods, views, and a feeling of really getting away from it all are highlights of this circuit.

Rangers recommend the walk described below as a good introduction to the Pogonip.

Directions to trailhead: In Santa Cruz, from the junction of Highway 1 and Highway 9, head north on Highway 9 exactly ⅔-mile and turn left on Golf Club Drive. Park in the lot at the corner.

The walk: Head up Golf Club Drive ¼-mile, passing under a railroad trestle, to the entrance to Pogonip. You'll walk along the back of Pogonip Club, a premier polo club in the 1930s and 1940s. After World War II, the facility became a social club. It's now closed.

Join Old Stables Trail, crossing a meadow and passing an unsigned junction with Pogonip Creek Trail. The trail joins Brayshaw Trail, a service road, and ascends to a junction with Spring Trail. Go right (north) to the handsome meadow at the junction with Ohlone Trail. From Haunted Meadow, those experienced with Pogonip pathways might improvise a return route via Haunted Meadow Trail or Lookout Trail, but first-timers will return the way they came.

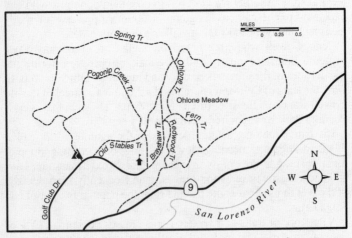

3. Monterey Bay

Before the 1849 gold rush and overnight rise of the city and port of San Francisco, Monterey was the political and commercial center of California. A waterfront walk of Monterey offers a glimpse backward at this time, and at other colorful periods of the city's history. Walkers will enjoy visiting Cannery Row, Fisherman's Wharf, and the world-renowned Monterey Bay Aquarium.

North of the city of Monterey is a diverse coastline that rewards the curious walker—beaches, bluff tops, and wetlands. Providing a dramatic backdrop to these northern beaches are some of the Central Coast's tallest dunes, handsomely shaped sand mounds that are habitat for a number of rare native plants and animals.

Elkhorn Slough, the largest wetland between Morro and San Francisco bays, is a critical rest stop and feeding ground for tens of thousands of migratory birds. Bird-watchers flock to the slough, where the record was established for the most bird species (116) sighted in a single day.

A visit to Point Lobos Reserve, in good weather or bad, is always memorable. Some of photographer Ansel Adams's greatest work was inspired by the wind-sculpted cypress, lonely sentinels perched at the edge of the continent. Landscape artist Francis McComas called Point Lobos "the greatest meeting of land and water in the world."

Moss Landing Wildlife Area
Marsh Trail

> **Terrain:** Salt marsh.
> **Highlights:** Bird-watching.
> **Distance:** To picnic area is 4½ miles round-trip.
> **Degree of difficulty:** Easy to moderate.

Elkhorn Slough, the Central California Coast's second-largest salt marsh, preserves crucial habitat for waterfowl. The north bank of the slough is protected within the confines of the 700-acre Moss Landing Wildlife Area.

Salt is a word to remember around here. In the late nineteenth century, the Monterey Bay Salt Company constructed salt ponds, harvesting the salt and supplying the Monterey and Moss Landing canneries. Today these former saltwater evaporation ponds host thousands of California brown pelicans.

The Moss Landing Wildlife Area, under the jurisdiction of the California Department of Fish and Wildlife, is managed differently than adjoining Elkhorn Slough National Estuarine Research Reserve. Waterfowl hunting is permitted.

Wildlife Area trails wind through various habitats around the slough: coastal salt marsh, freshwater ponds, oak woodland, and grassland.

Directions to trailhead: From Highway 1 at the highway bridge in Moss Landing, drive 1⁷⁄₁₀ miles north to a somewhat inconspicuous dirt road on the right that leads a short distance to the Moss Landing Wildlife Area parking lot.

For safety reasons, southbound travelers should continue past the entrance to the wildlife area to Struve Road, turn around, and come back on Highway 1 northbound.

The walk: The path crosses a low dike and soon reaches a signed junction. A side path (sometimes called West Trail or West Blind Trail) leads to the turn-of-the-century ponds where salt was harvested. Brown pelicans roost here in summer. The salt flats, all those pelicans, and the twin towers of the Moss Landing power plant in the background add up to a somewhat surreal scene.

Mostly level Marsh Trail travels along the slough's northwest shoreline and brings you to another side trail—leading to an overlook of the main channel of Elkhorn Slough.

The path turns a bit away from the slough through a rolling grassland environment. Cows graze on the adjacent private property. A couple of oak-shaded tables on a bluff high above the slough make a fine picnic area.

If you want to extend your hike, Marsh Trail continues a few more miles, skirting a native oak woodland and bending north to follow the main channel of Elkhorn Slough.

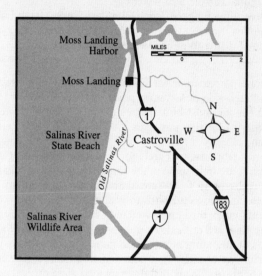

Elkhorn Slough

Long Valley, Five Fingers Loop Trails

> **Terrain:** Salt marsh.
> **Highlights:** Terrific bird-watching.
> **Distance:** Five Fingers Loop is 2 miles; South Marsh Loop
>   is 3 miles.
> **Degree of difficulty:** Easy to moderate.

Three words to remember at Elkhorn Slough: *birds, birds, birds.* From a slough-side observation point in 1983, the record was established for the most bird species (116) seen in a single day in North America. In all, more than 250 species have been sighted at the slough.

The birds, from snowy egrets to great blue herons to California clapper rails, are only some of the slough showstoppers. Fat worms and fast crabs—bird food—are abundant on the mudflats and are often as fascinating as the birds to visiting children.

Elkhorn Slough, the largest wetland between Morro Bay and San Francisco Bay, is a critical rest stop and feeding ground for tens of thousands of migratory birds. The slough, located halfway between Santa Cruz and Monterey, is believed to have received its name from the herds of tule elk that once roamed these coastal wetlands. Another guess is that the antlerlike shape of the slough prompted its name.

The 1,400-acre slough, officially the Elkhorn Slough National Estuarine Research Reserve, is managed by the California Department of Fish and Wildlife in partnership with the National Oceanic and Atmospheric Administration. A visitor center features interpretive displays and a book/gift shop. Elkhorn Slough and its visitor center are open Wednesday through Sunday only.

Three loop trails tour the slough, as well as adjacent oak woodland and grassland environments. From the visitor center, a paved path offers wheelchair access to a viewpoint.

The reserve's two westside loop trails—Long Valley and Five Fingers—are primarily upland trails through oak-dotted grassland; they do, however, touch the slough in a couple of places. If you have time for only one walk, take the South Marsh Loop Trail, which stays closer to the slough's shores.

Directions to trailhead: From Highway 1 in Moss Landing, turn east on Dolan Road and drive 3 miles. Turn left (north) and proceed 2 more miles to the entrance of Elkhorn Slough Reserve.

The walk: Long Valley Loop Trail forks left from the main path leading from the visitor center. A wooden dock provides a good viewpoint. Cresting a low rise, the trail reaches a junction with Five Fingers Loop Trail: fork left to make a second loop. (At Parsons Slough Overlook you'll probably figure out how Five Fingers Loop got its name.) When Five Fingers Loop Trail returns to the main preserve path, you can return to the visitor center or join South Marsh Loop Trail.

South Marsh Loop Trail briefly descends, approaching the abandoned barns of the old Elkhorn Dairy, then forks left, soon crossing a footbridge over the slough. Walking westward brings you to the primary channel of the slough. You can detour north across a dike bordering Whistle Stop Lagoon and view a couple of "Art in Nature" projects at an overlook of Elkhorn Slough channel. The trail passes a heron rookery and a eucalyptus woodland before angling back toward the visitor center.

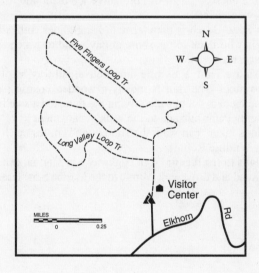

Marina State Beach

Dune Nature Trail

Terrain: Tall sand dunes.
Highlights: Excellent interpretive trail.
Distance: Nature trail with return via beach is ⅗-mile
   round-trip.
Degree of difficulty: Easy.

Providing a dramatic backdrop to Marina State Beach are some of
the Central Coast's tallest dunes, handsomely shaped sand mounds
that are habitat for a number of plants and animals. Rare native
flowers such as the Monterey paintbrush and the coast wallflower
brighten the dunes, where the black legless lizard and the ornate
shrew skitter about. These dune creatures and their habitat are threatened by the encroachment of non-native ice plant and, of course,
human developments.

Marina State Beach is popular with hang-glider enthusiasts and
with locals who flock to the shore at day's end to watch the often
colorful sunsets.

Dune Nature Trail, a ³⁄₁₀-mile interpretive pathway, explores the
dune ecosystem. The trail is mostly a wooden boardwalk linked
with "sand ladders." Signs identifying the flora and a swell view of
the Monterey Peninsula add to the walk's enjoyment.

Ambitious hikers can walk the shoreline 3½ miles north to Salinas River Wildlife Refuge.

Directions to trailhead: From Highway 1 in Marina, exit on Reservation Road and drive west ¼-mile to the Marina State Beach parking lot.

Salinas River State Beach

Dune Trail

> **Terrain:** Dunes, beach.
> **Highlights:** Visit Moss Landing, explore dunes.
> **Distance:** 2 miles round-trip.
> **Degree of difficulty:** Easy.

Mile-long Dune Trail explores some of Monterey Bay's intriguing sand dunes and links two coastal access points of Salinas River State Beach. The dunes back the state beach, a popular fishing spot.

East of the dunes are croplands and wetlands in the former Salinas River channel, which extends south from Moss Landing to the Salinas River Wildlife Area; in 1908, farmers diverted its course to create additional farmland.

Dune Trail begins south of the harbor of Moss Landing, often a surprisingly good place to watch for wildlife: sea otters paddle here and there; sea lions bask on a narrow finger of sand; pelicans are abundant in air and on land and in sea.

From the harbor, walkers can follow a ½-mile dirt road (closed to vehicles) south to the Salinas River State Beach access and parking area off Portrero Road, where Dune Trail officially begins.

Directions to trailhead: From Highway 1 at Moss Landing, exit on Portrero Road and follow it ½-mile to the parking lot at Salinas River State Beach.

Another trailhead is off Molera Road. Follow signed Monterey Dunes Way ½-mile to the beach.

Warning: Both trailheads have been the site of vehicle break-ins. Lock your car and take your valuables with you.

The walk: The path is over soft sand, seasonally colored by lupine, Indian paintbrush, and California poppy. Hikers get mostly inland views, though the path does crest a rise for a peek at the coast. A mile out, you have the choice of retracing your steps or returning via the beach.

Monterey Bay

Monterey Bay Recreation Trail

Terrain: Historic waterfront of Monterey.
Highlights: Cannery Row, Monterey State Historic Park,
  Monterey Bay Aquarium.
Distance: From Fisherman's Wharf to Monterey Bay Aquar-
  ium is 2 miles round-trip.
Degree of difficulty: Easy.

Before the 1849 gold rush and overnight rise of the city and port of
San Francisco, Monterey was the political and commercial center
of California. A waterfront walk of Monterey offers a glimpse backward at this time—and to other colorful periods of the city's history.

Monterey is probably most identified with its world-renowned
sardine-canning industry, but the city has hosted many other enterprises that reflect the diverse ethnic heritage of California. Monterey's storied shores have been the work site for Mexican custom
officials, Yankee traders, Portuguese whalers, and Chinese and Italian fishers.

As a supplement to this walk, which stays close to the waterfront,
be sure to venture downtown along the self-guided "Monterey Path
of History." This tour visits many of the buildings within Monterey
State Historic Park. Of particular interest to Central Coast history
buffs is the Old Whaling Station, a boardinghouse for whalers in
the 1850s, and the Allen Knight Maritime Museum, which features
exhibits of maritime and naval history. One museum highlight is
the 1887 Fresnel lens from the Point Sur Light Station.

This walk's destination, the Monterey Bay Aquarium, is open
daily from 10:00 A.M. to 6:00 P.M.

Directions to trailhead: From Highway 1, and from downtown
Monterey, signs direct you to "Fisherman's Wharf." There's parking in the municipal lot at the end of Alvarado Street.

The walk: Before heading for Fisherman's Wharf, also known as
Wharf Number One, check out Municipal Wharf, or Wharf Number Two. This utilitarian structure, built in 1926, serves Monterey's
commercial fishing fleet. Cranes, hoists, and forklifts unload the

fleet's catch, which can include squid, shrimp, salmon, sole, anchovy, and Pacific herring.

Fisherman's Wharf, built in 1870 by the Pacific Coast Steamship Company to serve cargo schooners, became a bustling adjunct to the canneries of Cannery Row during the 1930s. If you walk past the tourist shops, fish markets, and seafood restaurants, you can see sea lions frolicking below the pier. Beware of sea gulls flying overhead; they compete for the fish that tourists throw to the sea lions and pelicans.

Before heading around the bay to Cannery Row, detour across the plaza next to the wharf to see Custom House, the oldest public building on the California coast. When Mexico ruled California, custom duties were collected from foreign ships. The building now houses a collection of clothing, leather goods, and china typical of items imported through old Monterey.

Proceed through Shoreline Park on the Monterey Recreation Trail, a paved bicycle and pedestrian path. The level route follows the old railbed of the Del Monte Express, which from 1879 to 1972 carried passengers from San Francisco to Pebble Beach and Del Monte Lodge.

Stay on the pedestrian path along the waterfront to the Coast Guard Pier at the southeast end of Cannery Row. A rock jetty extending from the end of the pier is a favorite haul-out for sea lions.

The first fish-processing plant on what was to become Cannery Row was built in 1902. Canneries packaged food for human consumption. Reduction plants processed sardine by-products into fish meal or animal feed, and into oil used in manufacturing things such as paint and vitamins.

Peak sardine production was reached in 1945, the year John Steinbeck's *Cannery Row* was published. During the boom, the humble sardine supported an industry that crowded 23 canneries and 19 reduction plants along one mile of shoreline. Marine scientists warned of overfishing, and in 1951 the fish all but vanished from California's waters. Some evidence now suggests that the sardines are making a comeback.

Follow Cannery Row past a mix of abandoned canneries, luxury hotels, restaurants, tourist shops, and a bust of John Steinbeck. As Steinbeck, on a return visit many years after publication of his novel, summed up Cannery Row: "They fish for tourists now."

The $50 million Monterey Bay Aquarium, which opened in 1984, is one of the world's finest. The state-of-the-art exhibits and display tanks are superb. Particularly noteworthy for admirers of California's

Central Coast is the fact that almost all displays emphasize the rich underwater world of Monterey Bay.

One aquarium highlight is a mature kelp forest. A multitude of fish swim past tall stands of giant kelp, one of the world's fastest-growing plants. Another absorbing exhibit is the Monterey Bay Tank, which re-creates the world of a submarine canyon, complete with sharks and brightly colored fish.

Beyond the aquarium, the Monterey Recreation Trail leads past rows of Victorian houses to the wind-sculpted cypress trees atop Lover's Point. From the point's grassy picnic area, you can enjoy a great view of the southern sweep of Monterey Bay.

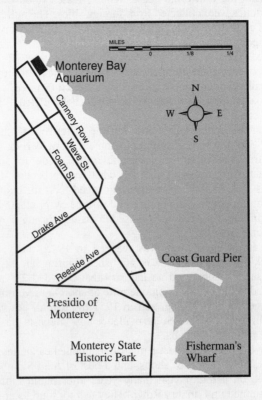

Asilomar State Beach

Asilomar Coast Trail

> **Terrain:** Dunes, rich tide pools, broad beach.
> **Highlights:** Restored dune ecosystem, historic Asilomar
> Conference Center.
> **Distance:** ½-mile to 2 miles round-trip.
> **Degree of difficulty:** Easy.

Asilomar State Beach, located on the southwest shores of Pacific Grove, packs a lot of interest into a mile of coastline: a restored dune ecosystem, rocky coves, a broad sand beach. Add a visit to the historic Asilomar Conference Center and you have a walk to remember.

Bordering the west side of the conference center are white sand dunes vegetatively restored to their original condition. A boardwalk provides close-up views of this living example of plant succession: just inland from the water, "pioneer" species of sand verbena and beach sagewort have taken hold; these colonizers created soil conditions acceptable for larger plants such as coffeeberry and coyote brush to thrive; ultimately Monterey pine and coast live oak will succeed.

The conference center at Asilomar (pronounced *ah-seel-o-mar,* derived from the Spanish to suggest "refuge by the sea") was founded by the YWCA for use as a summer retreat in 1913. Architect Julia Morgan, who would later gain worldwide fame as the designer of Hearst Castle, was commissioned to plan the original buildings.

Asilomar Conference Center now belongs to the state and is managed by a concessionaire. Trail advocates take note: Asilomar is the spring gathering place for the annual meeting of the California Recreational Trails Committee, a group that promotes trails statewide.

Asilomar Coast Trail extends a mile along the length of the state beach. From the trail, several side paths fork to tide pools and pocket beaches. Sea otters, sea lions, and seals are sometimes seen from vantage points along the trail. In winter, scan the horizon for migrating California gray whales.

From the coast, walkers can follow the boardwalk across dunes to the Asilomar Conference Center, a national historic landmark set in the piney woods.

Directions to trailhead: From Highway 1 between Carmel and Monterey, turn west on Highway 68 (which becomes Sunset Drive) and follow it to the beach. If you're in the Cannery Row area, follow Ocean View Boulevard west and south along the coast.

You can begin this walk opposite Asilomar Conference Center or at the north end of Asilomar State Beach just south of the Sunset Drive–Jewell Avenue intersection.

Jacks Peak County Park

Skyline, Iris, Rhus Trails

> **Terrain:** Monterey pine–forested hills.
> **Highlights:** Grand views from high point of Monterey Peninsula.
> **Distance:** Skyline Nature Trail is a ⅘-mile loop; return via Iris and Rhus trails is 2⅘ miles round-trip.
> **Degree of difficulty:** Easy.

The Monterey Peninsula's high point, Jacks Peak, offers terrific vistas of Monterey and Carmel bays.

Jacks Peak is forested with the largest remaining native Monterey pine grove in the world. (Only three other native stands exist: near Cambria, at Santa Cruz, and on Guadalupe Island some 200 miles off the coast of Baja California.) While the fast-growing Monterey pine has been successfully transplanted across California and around the world, there is something special about visiting the conifer in its native habitat.

Jacks Peak and Jacks Park honor Scottish immigrant David Jacks, a successful nineteenth-century businessman, dairy owner, and land speculator. Jacks is best remembered today, however, for his "Monterey Jack" cheese, the only native California cheese.

About 10 miles of trail meander through Jacks Peak County Park. Paths visit the Monterey pines, as well as oak woodland and wildflower-dotted meadows.

For a quick tour and a view, take the Skyline Nature Trail, a ⅘-mile loop keyed to an interpretive pamphlet. The quick route to the top is by way of Jacks Peak Trail (⅗-mile). The summit of Jacks Peak offers glorious views of the Carmel coast and valley and the Santa Lucia Mountains of the Big Sur backcountry; it does not, however, provide good views of Monterey Bay, which is better observed from the lower slopes of the peak.

Directions to trailhead: From Highway 1 in Monterey, take Highway 68 east 1½ miles toward Salinas. Turn right on Olmsted Road and drive another 1½ miles to Jacks Peak Drive, which travels a mile to the entrance of Jacks Peak County Park. Day-use fees are two dollars per vehicle Monday through Thursday, three dollars per vehicle Friday through Sunday.

The park is open daily from 10:30 A.M. to 7:30 P.M. Hikers preferring an earlier start may park along Jacks Peak Drive below the gated park entry. It's about a 15-minute uphill walk on Jacks Peak Drive to the park-entry kiosk.

From the park's entry kiosk, turn right on Pine Road and follow it to its end at Jacks Peak Parking Area.

The walk: Begin on Skyline Nature Trail, which makes a counterclockwise circle of the mountain. An interpretive pamphlet, available at the trailhead, points out bird life, geology, and Monterey pine–forest ecology.

Not far from the start, a vista point offers an excellent panorama (on fog-free days): Fisherman's Wharf, downtown Monterey, Cannery Row, Monterey Bay Aquarium, the Marina State Beach sand dunes, and Moss Landing.

From the nature trail, Jacks Peak Trail branches the short distance to the top of Jacks Peak.

Continue on Skyline Nature Trail as it rounds the peak, descending and contouring south, then east to intersect Iris Trail. Iris Trail descends Jacks's forested eastern slopes, then turns north to meet Rhus Trail. Turn left and head west back to Skyline Nature Trail. Follow the nature trail back to the trailhead.

Carmel River State Beach
Carmel River Beach Trail

> **Terrain:** Sandbar, river mouth, lagoon.
> **Highlights:** Wild ocean side of quaint Carmel; bird sanctuary.
> **Distance:** 2 miles round-trip.
> **Degree of difficulty:** Easy.

Carmel River, which arises high on the eastern slopes of the Santa Lucia Mountains and empties into the sea just south of Carmel, is a river of many moods. Some of its forks, when swollen by winter and spring rains, can be capricious, frothy waterways as they course through the Ventana Wilderness.

Tamed by Los Padres Dam on the northern boundary of the national forest, the river's descent through Carmel Valley is relatively peaceful. At its mouth, too, the Carmel River has differing moods and appearances. Around the month of May, a sandbar forms, turning the river mouth into a tranquil lagoon. During winter, the river bursts through the berm and rushes to the sea. Steelhead trout swim upriver to spawn.

At the north end of Carmel River State Beach is a brackish lagoon where shorebirds feed. Carmel River Lagoon and Wetlands Natural Reserve is here, and even the most casual bird-watcher will be impressed by the abundance of waterfowl. Ducks, mallards, and coots patrol the lagoon. Egrets and herons stand amongst the reeds. Hawks hover overhead. Bring your binoculars.

This walk explores the river mouth, then travels the length of Carmel River State Beach to a point, just north of Point Lobos, named Monastery Beach after the Carmelite Monastery located just across Highway 1 from the shore.

Directions to trailhead: During the summer and autumn months, the sandy berm at the mouth of the Carmel River provides a fine path between river and sea. At this time of year, you can start this walk at the north end of Carmel River State Beach. From Highway 1, just south of the town of Carmel, turn west on Rio Road. When you reach Santa Lucia Street, turn left, then proceed five more blocks to Carmelo Street. Turn left and follow this road to the beach.

You can also start at the south end of Carmel River State Beach, easily accessible from Highway 1.

The walk: Follow the shoreline down coast over the sandy berm. In places, the route is rocky, the domain of nervous crabs, who scatter at your approach. You will surely notice the iceplant-lined path above the beach; save this path for your return trip.

After rounding a minor point and passing some wind-bent Monterey cypress, you will arrive at Monastery Beach—also known as San Jose Creek Beach, after the creek that empties onto the northern end of the beach. With the chimes from the nearby monastery ringing in your ears, you might be lulled into thinking Monastery Beach is a tranquil place. But it's not. The surf is rough and the beach drops sharply off into the sea. Even the most experienced swimmers should be ultracautious.

For a slightly different return route, take the state beach service road, which farther north becomes a trail. This dirt road/trail, just before reaching the lagoon, climbs a small hill where a large cross is implanted. The cross was erected by the Carmel Mission in 1944, and is similar to the one put here by the 1769 Portola expedition in order to signal the Spanish ship that was to resupply them. Unfortunately, the expedition did not realize how close it was to its intended destination—Monterey Bay— and turned back south.

From the cross, follow a path downslope and intersect another path that leads along the south bank of the Carmel River. Follow the berm and beach back to the trailhead.

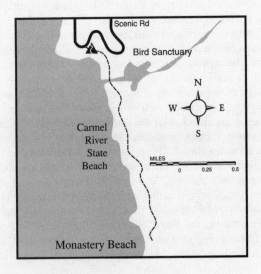

Point Lobos State Reserve

Cypress Grove Trail

> **Terrain:** Pine and cypress woodland, coastal bluffs.
> **Highlights:** Some call it the greatest meeting of land and
>   water in the world.
> **Distance:** ¾-mile round-trip.
> **Degree of difficulty:** Easy.

Sometimes it's the tranquil moments at Point Lobos that you remember: black-tailed deer moving through the forest, the fog-
wrapped cypress trees. And sometimes it's nature's more boisterous
moments that you recall: the bark of sea lions at Sea Lion Point, the
sea thundering against the cliffs.

A visit to Point Lobos State Reserve, in good weather and bad,
is always memorable. Some of photographer Ansel Adams's greatest work was inspired by the wind-sculpted cypress, lonely sentinels perched at the edge of the continent. Landscape artist Francis
McComas called Point Lobos "the greatest meeting of land and
water in the world."

At Point Lobos, the Monterey cypress makes a last stand. Botanists
believe that during Pleistocene times, some half-million years ago
when the climate was wetter and cooler than it is now, huge forests
of cypress grew along the coast—indeed, throughout North America. When the world's climate warmed, the cypress retreated to a
few damp spots. Nowadays, the grove at Point Lobos and another
across Carmel Bay at Cypress Point are the only two native stands
in existence.

The Monterey cypress, with the help of human beings, can cross
hot and dry regions and become established in cool areas elsewhere. In fact, this rare conifer is easily grown from seed and has
been successfully distributed all over the world, so it's puzzling
why the tree's natural range is so restricted.

Cypress Grove Trail, a ¾-mile loop, visits Allan Memorial Grove,
which honors A. M. Allan, who, in the early years of this century,
helped preserve Point Lobos from resort developers. When Point
Lobos became a reserve in 1933, Allan's family gave the cypress
grove to the state.

The trail passes near The Pinnacle, the northernmost point in the reserve. Winds off the Pacific really batter this point and the exposed trees. To combat the wind, the trees adopt a survival response called buttressing: a narrow part of the trunk faces the wind while the trunk grows thicker on the other side in order to brace itself. The wind-sculpted trunks and wind-shaped foliage give the cypress their fantastic shapes.

Cypress Grove Trail offers great tree-framed views of Carmel Bay and Monterey Peninsula. Offshore are the rocky islands near Sea Lion Point. The Spaniards called the domain of these creatures Punto de los Lobos Marinos—Point of the Sea Wolves. You'll probably hear the barking of the sea lions before you see them.

Directions to trailhead: Point Lobos State Reserve is 3 miles south of Carmel just off Highway 1. There is a state park day-use fee. Both Cypress Grove Trail and North Shore Trail depart from the northwest end of Cypress Grove parking area.

Photographers, artists, writers—and hikers—have long been inspired by the natural drama at Point Lobos.

Point Lobos State Reserve

North Shore Trail

Terrain: Pine and cypress woodland, coastal bluffs.
Highlights: Some call it the greatest meeting of land and
water in the world.
Distance: 3 miles or more.
Degree of difficulty: Easy.

North Shore Trail meanders through groves of Monterey pine, less
celebrated than the Monterey cypress but nearly as rare. Native
stands of the fog-loving, three-needled pine grow in only a few
place in California.

Watchers of the late, late show and admirers of spooky beauty
will enjoy the shrouds of pale green lichen hanging from the dead
branches of the Monterey pines. Lichen, which conducts the business of life as a limited partnership of algae and fungi, is not a par-
asite and does not hurt the tree. It's believed that the presence of
lichen is an indication of extremely good air quality.

North Shore Trail wanders through Monterey pines and offers
terrific coastal panoramas. The trail also gives a bird's-eye view of
Guillemot Island. A variety of birds nest atop this large offshore
rock and others. Pigeon guillemots, cormorants, and gulls are some
of the birds you might see.

As you hike by Whalers Cove, you'll probably see divers entering the Point Lobos Underwater Reserve, set aside in 1960 as
America's first such reserve. Divers explore the 100-foot-high kelp
forests in Whalers and Blue Fish Coves. Mineral rich waters from
the nearby 1,000-foot-deep Carmel Submarine Canyon upwell to
join the more shallow waters of the coves.

The reserve has an excellent interpretive program. Docent-led
walks explore the trails and tide pools. Ask rangers or visit the
park's information station to learn about scheduled nature walks.

Directions to trailhead: Point Lobos State Reserve is 3 miles
south of Carmel just off Highway 1. There is a state park day-use
fee. Both North Shore Trail and Cypress Grove Trail depart from
the northwest end of Cypress Grove parking area.

Big Sur's rugged coastline is one of California's most dramatic locales.

4. Big Sur Coast

Big Sur means different things to different people. To hardy hikers it's the challenging Ventana Wilderness backcountry. To others it's the hamlet of Big Sur with its post office, roadside businesses and campgrounds, lodging and information station.

For the motorist, Coast Highway from Carmel to the Monterey–San Luis Obispo county line has long been regarded as one of the world's great drives. In 1965 this stretch of Highway 1 was designated California's first scenic highway.

But the highway, noble engineering feat that it was, great road that it is, only gets you so close to the Big Sur coast. While more than three million visitors a year pass through Big Sur and receive at least a little inspiration from the seascapes seen through their windshields, most of these travelers leave knowing no more about Big Sur than when they first arrived.

Certainly you can do as countless others have done: stop your car for a few minutes at a viewpoint and look down at the surf surging over the rocks. But a more intimate connection with this coast can be gained by walking to and along the shore, getting close-up views of otters grabbing mussels off the rocks or cormorants diving for fish. A little effort yields big rewards: wildflowers, wildlife, and wild beaches hidden from the highway.

Some of Big Sur's best coastline is preserved within state parks: Garrapata, Andrew Molera, Point Sur Light Station, Pfeiffer Big Sur, and Julia Pfeiffer Burns. Los Padres National Forest, one of the nation's very few forests to boast ocean frontage, also has some beaches, campgrounds, and inspiring coastal pathways.

Soberanes Point

Soberanes Point Trail

> **Terrain:** Bold headland, coastal bluffs.
> **Highlights:** Discovering overlooked park, dramatic shore-
>   line.
> **Distance:** 1¾ miles round-trip.
> **Degree of difficulty:** Easy.

Overlooked and underrated would be one way to characterize the dramatic shoreline of Garrapata State Park. Its neighbor to the north, Point Lobos State Reserve, often billed as "the greatest meeting of land and sea in the world," deservedly gets a lot of attention. And Andrew Molera, Garrapata's sister state park to the south, boasts the Big Sur River and a walk-in campground that attracts visitors from around the world.

What Garrapata offers is some of the Central Coast's most striking coastline—hidden beaches, rocky coves, and bluffs carpeted with native wildflowers and introduced ice plant. Another lure is wonderful wildlife-watching. Sea otters and sea lions bask on Lobos Rocks just offshore. Seabirds such as oystercatchers and cormorants glide over the waves. Garrapata's bluffs are excellent vantage points from which to observe California gray whales on their annual winter migration.

Garrapata Beach is a ½-mile sand strand accessible by a short ¼-mile trail that begins at Gate 32 on the ocean side of Highway 1.

Be extra cautious on Garrapata's sandy shores and rocky points. The coast here is known for its "rogue" waves—ocean swells that have swept the unwary off their feet, and in some cases to their deaths.

The best-marked paths in the park surround Soberanes Point, a bold headland that terminates in a roundish ridge known as Whale Peak.

Directions to trailhead: From Highway 1, some 7 miles south of Carmel, look for Gate 13 on the west side of the highway. Park in a safe manner off the highway. Soberanes Point Trail shares a trailhead with Soberanes Canyon Trail located on the east side of Highway 1.

The walk: Head south, visiting some windswept cypress, then walking onto the bluffs to an unsigned junction. Head right toward Soberanes Point, passing along the coastal side of Whale Peak. Go right at the next junction, dropping toward a second point. You'll contour to the Coast Highway side of Whale Peak.

A mile from the trailhead, an inviting ¼-mile connector path takes you to Whale Peak Saddle, where short footpaths lead in turn to the north and south summits of the peak. From both summits, the hiker may enjoy grand coastal views north to Carmel's Yankee Point and south to Point Sur.

Return to Soberanes Point Trail, which heads south, rejoining the first ¹⁄₁₀-mile of trail and returning to the trailhead.

Garrapata State Park

Rocky Ridge, Soberanes Canyon Trails

Terrain: Steep Santa Lucia Mountains.
Highlights: Grand Big Sur coastal views, redwoods.
Distance: 7 miles round-trip with 1,200-foot elevation gain.
Degree of difficulty: Moderate to strenuous.
Precautions: Steep trail, poison oak; *garrapata* means tick in Spanish—watch out for them.

Undeveloped and usually overlooked, Garrapata State Park offers a lot of Big Sur in a compact area. The park features 2 miles (probably closer to 4 miles counting the twists and turns) of spectacular coastline and a steep sampling of the Santa Lucia Mountains.

Rocky Ridge Trail quickly leaves Highway 1 behind and offers far-reaching views of the Santa Lucia Mountains and the sea. A grand loop of the state park can be made by returning to the trailhead by way of redwood-lined Soberanes Canyon Trail.

The name Soberanes is linked with the early Spanish exploration of California. Soldier José María Soberanes marched up the coast to Monterey with the Gaspar de Portola expedition of 1769. Seven years later, Soberanes served as a guide for Juan Bautista de Anza, whose party pushed north to San Francisco Bay. Grandson José Antonio Ezequiel Soberanes acquired the coastal bluff and magnificent backcountry that became known as the Soberanes Ranch.

Garrapata State Park offers a variety of hiking options. The coast lover can loop around aptly named Whale Peak, which is not only cetacean-shaped but offers good views of migrating gray whales from about March through April. The whales can be seen swimming—usually fairly close to shore—as they head back to Arctic waters. The most popular whale-watching spot in the park, however, is Soberanes Point. Bring your binoculars.

Rocky Ridge Trail will be more enjoyable for the gung-ho hiker than for the novice. The trail ascends very steeply toward Rocky Ridge. Then, after gaining the ridge, hikers must descend an extremely steep mile (we're talking about a 20 to 30 percent grade here) to connect to Soberanes Canyon Trail.

The leg-weary, or those simply looking for an easier walk, will simply stroll through the redwoods of Soberanes Canyon and not attempt Rocky Ridge Trail.

Directions to trailhead: Garrapata State Park is 7 miles south of Carmel Valley Road, off Highway 1 in Carmel. There's a highway turnout at mileage marker 65.8.

The walk: From the gate on the east side of Highway 1, walk inland over a dirt road to a nearby barn, then a wee bit farther to cross Soberanes Creek and reach a trail junction. Soberanes Canyon heads east along the creek, but Rocky Ridge–bound hikers will keep with the closed road, heading north and dipping in and out of a gully.

Hikers rapidly leave the highway behind as the path climbs the rugged slopes, which are dotted with black sage, golden yarrow, and bush lupine. The route uses few switchbacks as it ascends 1,435-foot Rocky Ridge. From atop the ridge are good views to the east of Soberanes Creek watershed, to the west of Soberanes Point, and to the north of Carmel and the Monterey Peninsula.

The route contours eastward around the ridge. To the north is the steep canyon cut by Malpaso Creek. After leveling out for a time, the grassy path reaches a small cow pond, then begins to descend over steep but pastoral terrain.

The trail is cut by cattle paths, a reminder of a century of grazing. The route plunges very steeply down the bald north wall of Soberanes Canyon. The mile-long killer descent finally ends when you intersect Soberanes Canyon Trail and begin descending, much more gently, to the west.

Soberanes Canyon Trail stays close to the creek and enters the redwoods. Western sword fern, redwood sorrel, blackberry bushes, and Douglas irises decorate the path.

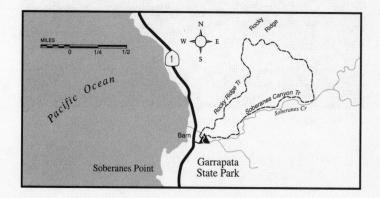

Near the mouth of the canyon, the trail becomes gentler. Willow, watercress, and horsetail line the lower reaches of Soberanes Creek. Soon after passing some out-of-place mission cacti, brought north from Mexico by Spanish missionaries, hikers return to the trailhead.

Tour Point Sur's historic light station, and enjoy the view from the top.

Point Sur Light Station State Historic Park

Point Sur Lightstation Trail

Terrain: Dramatic Big Sur bluffs.
Highlights: Century-old lighthouse, guided tour.
Distance: ½-mile guided walk.
Degree of difficulty: Easy.

During the nineteenth century, when coastal roads were few and poor, most cargo was transported by ship. Ships traveled close to shore to take advantage of the protection offered by bay and point. This heavy coastal trade—and its dangers—prompted the U.S. Lighthouse Service Board to establish a series of lighthouses located about 60 miles apart along California's coast.

Point Sur had been the death of many ships, and mariners had been petitioning for a beacon for many years when the government in 1885 appropriated $50,000 to construct a light station. The Point Sur light joined already existing lights at Piedras Blancas and Pigeon Point, located, respectively, 60 miles south and 60 miles north of Point Sur.

The first Point Sur light, which became operational in 1889, utilized one of the famed Fresnel lenses designed by French physicist Augustin-Jean Fresnel. A whale-oil lantern was the first light source. In later years kerosene fueled the operation. Soot problems from the not-very-clean-burning kerosene kept the keepers busy polishing the glass and worrying about surprise visits from supervisors who conducted "white glove" inspections.

The lighthouse became fully automated in 1975. The original light, visible for 23 miles out to sea, is now on display in the Maritime Museum of Monterey.

The century-old stone buildings, when viewed from Highway 1, are intriguing; they're even more so when seen up close on one of the tours conducted by volunteer docents. While the station undergoes restoration, the only way to see the facility—the only intact light station with accompanying support buildings on the California coast—is by guided tour.

The tour includes the lighthouse itself, the keepers' houses, the blacksmith shop, and the barn, where livestock was kept. You'll learn the fascinating story of the isolated life lived by the 4 keepers and their families.

Docent-led tours are currently offered on weekends and on some Wednesdays: Saturdays 10:00 A.M. and 2:00 P.M., Sundays 10:00 A.M., and Wednesdays 10:00 A.M., weather permitting. There's a fee for the tours, which have a limited number of slots—available on a first-come, first-served basis. Suggestion: arrive early. For more information: (408) 625–4419.

The walk to the lighthouse is interesting for more than historical reasons. Geology buffs will call the path to the light the "Tombolo Trail"; a tombolo, rare on the California coast, is a sandbar connecting an island to the mainland.

The view from atop the 360-foot-high basaltic rock is superb. You're eyeball-to-eyeball with the gulls and cormorants. To the south is False Sur, named for its confusing resemblance to Point Sur when viewed from the sea.

In 1980 Point Sur Light Station was designated a state historic landmark, and in 1984 the U.S. Department of the Interior turned it over to the California Department of Parks and Recreation. The old Lighthouse Service Board was long ago absorbed by the U.S. Coast Guard, and the kerosene lamp and steam-driven warning whistle have been replaced by a computer-directed electric beam and radio beacon, but Point Sur Light Station, as it has for a century, continues to warn ships of the treacherous Big Sur coast.

Directions to trailhead: Point Sur Light Station State Historic Park is located on the west side of Highway 1, some 19 miles south of Carmel and ¼-mile north of Point Sur Naval Facility.

Until the light station was installed, the Big Sur Coast was the death of many ships.

Andrew Molera State Park

Beach, Headlands Trails

> **Terrain:** Meadows, rugged coastal bluffs.
> **Highlights:** Big Sur River mouth, redwoods, dramatic coast.
> **Distance:** 3 miles round-trip.
> **Degree of difficulty:** Beach Trail is an easy family walk.

Mountains, meadows, and the mouth of Big Sur River are some of the highlights of a walk through Andrew Molera State Park, the largest state park along the Big Sur coast.

More than 20 miles of trails weave through the park and its diverse ecosystems. You can hike along the bluffs overlooking 3 miles of beach and climb through meadows and oak woodland. At the river mouth are a shallow lagoon and a beautiful sandy beach.

In 1855 Yankee fur trader Juan Bautista Roger Cooper acquired this land, formerly part of the Mexican land grant Rancho del Sur. Acquaintances of his day—and historians of today—speculate that Cooper used his "Ranch of the South" as a landing spot, bringing cargo ashore at the Big Sur River mouth to avoid the high custom fees of Monterey Harbor.

Grandson Andrew Molera, who inherited the ranch, had a successful dairy operation. His Monterey Jack cheese was particularly prized. He was a hospitable fellow, popular with neighbors who camped along the river while awaiting shipments of supplies from San Francisco.

A good leg-stretcher walk is to take Beach Trail to the beach at the mouth of the Big Sur River, then return via Creamery Meadow Trail. Beach Trail and a number of other park roads are old dirt roads that allow side-by-side walking, thus appealing to sociable hikers.

In summer, you'll see surfers heading for the beach. You may also hear a number of foreign languages en route. The state park's walk-in campground is very popular with European visitors.

A longer tour of the park can be made via the Bluff, Panorama, and Ridge trails. The coastal views from these trails are magnificent.

Note that the round-trip loop described below relies on seasonal (late spring to early fall) footbridges. At other times, you'll have to make this trip an out-and-back or get your feet (and possibly much more) wet by crossing the river.

Directions to trailhead: Andrew Molera State Park is just off Highway 1, some 21 miles south of Carmel.

The walk: From the parking lot, cross the Big Sur River on the seasonal footbridge. Walk 100 yards or so along a broad path that soon splits. Bear right onto Beach Trail. (The left fork joins Creamery Meadow Trail, an ideal return route for those who like loop trails.) The path stays near the river, whose banks are crowded with thimbleberry and blackberry, honeysuckle vines, willow, and bay laurel.

At ³/₁₀-mile, you'll pass through the park's campground. A side trail leads to Cooper Cabin, an 1861 redwood structure that's the oldest building on Big Sur's coast.

At the river mouth is a small beach and shallow lagoon frequented by sanderlings, willets, and many more shorebirds. A short path (Headlands Trail) leads above the beach to Molera Point, where you can watch for whales (January through April) or passing ships. The beach to the south is walkable at low tide.

Loop around the point and then either return the same way or by way of Creamery Meadows Trail on the south side of the Big Sur River.

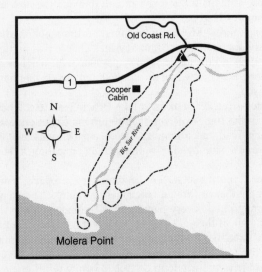

Andrew Molera State Park

Beach, Bluff, Panorama, Ridge Trails

Terrain: Meadows, rugged coastal bluffs.
Highlights: Big Sur River mouth, redwoods, dramatic coast.
Distance: 9½-mile loop with 1,000-foot elevation gain.
Degree of difficulty: Moderate to strenuous.

As the largest state park (4,800 acres) on the Big Sur coast, Andrew Molera offers the hiker access to broad bluffs, redwood-shaded canyons, and high ridge tops. Depending on time, inclination, and creative route-planning, a short, medium-sized, or lengthy loop can be made through the big park.

One of my favorite loops, a 9½-mile jaunt, links a half-dozen paths and provides a memorable tour: the Big Sur River; the bluffs above Molera Beach; and steep, grassy ridge tops that afford vistas of the coast as well as Ventana Wilderness peaks.

Note that the round-trip loop described below relies on seasonal (late spring to early fall) footbridges. At other times, you'll have to get your feet (and possibly much more) wet by crossing the Big Sur River.

Directions to trailhead: Andrew Molera State Park is just off Highway 1, 21 miles south of Carmel.

The walk: From the parking lot, cross the Big Sur River on the seasonal footbridge. Walk 100 yards of so along a broad path that soon splits. Bear right onto Beach Trail. (The left fork joins Creamery Meadow Trail, an ideal return route for those who like short loop trails.) The trail stays near the river, whose banks are crowded with thimbleberry and blackberry, honeysuckle vines, willow, and bay laurel.

At ³⁄₁₀-mile, you pass through the park's campground. A side trail leads to Cooper Cabin, an 1861 redwood structure that's the oldest building on Big Sur's coast.

At the river mouth is a small beach and shallow lagoon frequented by sanderlings, willets, and many more shorebirds. A short path (Headlands Trail) leads above the beach to Molera Point, where you can watch for whales (January through April) or passing ships. The beach to the south is walkable at low tide.

Loop around the point and then cross the summer footbridge over the Big Sur River. You'll follow the upper part of the beach, climb the bluffs, and head south to a junction with Bluff Trail and Ridge Trail.

Wide Bluff Trail, an old road, heads south over the almost level bluffs, a marine terrace cloaked in grasses and coastal scrub. Summer-blooming lizardtail blankets the terrace in yellow. Bluff Trail reaches a junction with Spring Trail, which offers a ¼-mile route to Molera Beach. (A picnic on the beach and a return to the trailhead from here would add up to a 6-mile round-trip hike.)

About 1¾ miles from the mouth of the Big Sur River, Bluff Trail gives way to Panorama Trail, a more rigorous path that soon drops into a deep gully, then climbs steeply up a ridge where wind-stunted redwoods cling to life. The path continues climbing toward the southern boundary of the park, reaching a junction with Ridge Trail at about 5½ miles from the trailhead. A bench offers a place to take it easy and eat your lunch. Your rewards for gaining about 900 feet in elevation are great views of the state park, the coast to the south, and triangular-shaped Cone Peak, one of the high points of the Santa Lucia Mountains.

Ridge Trail begins its long (nearly 4-mile) descent northwest along the park's main ridge. You'll pass through an oak grove, then a tan oak–redwood forest, before emerging onto the trail's more characteristic open, grassy slopes. Hidden Trail offers a shortcut to River Trail and back to the trailhead.

Ridge Trail continues back to the coast, where you can retrace your steps by taking Beach Trail to the trailhead or return via River Trail on the south side of the Big Sur River.

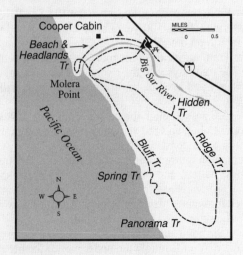

Pfeiffer Beach

Pfeiffer Beach Trail

Terrain: Isolated beach, sea stacks, blowholes.
Highlights: Big Sur coastline at its most magnificent.
Distance: To Pfeiffer Beach is ¾-mile round-trip.
Degree of difficulty: Easy.

Los Padres is one of only three national forests in America with ocean frontage. Named for a pioneer family, Pfeiffer is a secluded white sand beach facing a turbulent sea, which sends awesome waves crashing through blowholes in the rocks.

Many scenes from the *The Sandpiper,* with Elizabeth Taylor and Richard Burton, were filmed here. The magic of motion pictures gave us a calm beach where small boats landed easily. Big Sur residents laugh every time this movie is shown on late-night TV.

With its hazardous surf and gusty winds, Pfeiffer Beach cannot be said to be a comfortable stretch of coastline; it is, however, a magnificent one.

Directions to trailhead: Driving south, a mile south of Pfeiffer Big Sur State Park, take the second right-hand turn off Highway 1 (west). Sycamore Canyon Road is a sharp downhill turn. Follow the narrow, winding, and sometimes washed-out road 2 miles to the Forest Service parking area.

The walk: Follow the wide, sandy path and boardwalk leading from the parking lot through the cypress trees. Sycamore Creek empties into a small lagoon near the beach.

Marvel at the sea stacks, blowholes, and caves, and try to find a place out of the wind to eat your lunch. The more ambitious may pick their way northward for a mile, over rocks and around a point to a second crescent-shaped beach.

Pfeiffer Big Sur State Park

Valley View Trail

Terrain: Redwood slopes of Santa Lucia Mountains.
Highlights: Waterfall, classic Big Sur.
Distance: From Big Sur Lodge to Pfeiffer Falls, Valley
   View, is 2 miles round-trip with 200-foot elevation gain.
Degree of difficulty: Easy.

For most visitors, Big Sur means Pfeiffer Big Sur State Park. The park—and its brief but popular trail system—is dominated by the Big Sur River, which meanders through redwood groves on its way to the Pacific Ocean, 5 miles away.

John Pfeiffer, for whom the park was named, homesteaded 160 acres of mountainous terrain between Sycamore Canyon and the Big Sur River. In 1884 he moved into a cabin perched above the Big Sur River gorge. (You can see the reconstructed "Homestead Cabin," located on the park's Gorge Trail.) John Pfeiffer sold and donated some of his ranch land to the state in the 1930s, and it became the nucleus of the state park.

This walk, which follows the Pfeiffer Falls and Valley View trails, is an easy leg-stretcher suitable for the whole family. It visits Pfeiffer Falls and offers a good introduction to the delights of the state park.

Directions to trailhead: Pfeiffer Big Sur State Park is located off Highway 1, 26 miles south of Carmel and 2 miles south of the hamlet of Big Sur. Beyond the entry booth, turn left at the stop sign, then veer right (uphill). Very soon, you'll find some day-use parking. A much larger parking area is located near the store and restaurant at the bottom of the hill.

The walk: From the signed trailhead, follow the path to Pfeiffer Falls. Very shortly, on your left, you'll spot a trail heading left to Valley View; this will be your return route. The walk continues under stately redwoods and meanders along with Pfeiffer-Redwood Creek.

You'll soon ascend a redwood stairway to a junction with Oak Grove Trail, which leads rightward 1½ miles through oak and madrone woodland to the Mount Manuel Trail. Stay left at this junction and follow Pfeiffer Falls Trail through the forest and past a second branch of the Valley View Trail.

A stairway leads to an observation platform at the base of the falls. Pfeiffer-Redwood Creek cascades over a 40-foot precipice to a small grotto.

After enjoying the falls, descend the stairway and bear right on the Valley View Trail, which leaves the redwoods and ascends into a woodland of tanbark oak and coast live oak.

At a signed junction, turn right and follow the pathway along a minor ridge to a lookout. The Pacific Ocean pounding the Point Sur headlands and the Big Sur River valley are part of the fine view.

Backtrack along Valley View Trail and at the first junction stay right and descend on Pfeiffer Falls Trail back to Pfeiffer-Redwood Canyon. Another right at the canyon bottom brings you back to the trailhead.

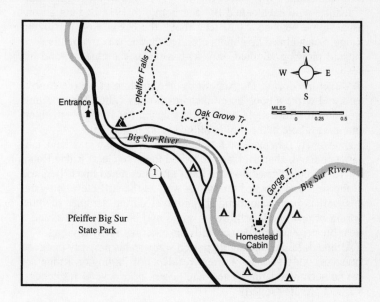

Partington Ridge

De Angulo Trail

> **Terrain:** Steep grassy slopes, tan-oak woodland.
> **Highlights:** Sweeping ocean and mountain views.
> **Distance:** From Highway 1 to Coast Ridge Road is 7 miles round-trip with 2,700-foot elevation gain.
> **Degree of difficulty:** Moderate to strenuous.

Jaime de Angulo was one of the most eccentric of the rugged individualists who have called Big Sur home. In 1914 he built an unusual home perched 2,000 feet above the ocean atop Partington Ridge. Scandalized neighbors reported that he was frequently seen outside plowing, clothed only with a red neckerchief around his head.

A onetime doctor, De Angulo studied the lore of Native Americans and wrote a book about their mythology called *Indian Tales*. He cooked native-style over a fire ring on his living-room floor, chopping a hole in the roof to allow smoke to escape.

De Angulo Trail leads up Partington Ridge through grassland, tan-oak woodland, chaparral, and redwood forest to Coast Ridge Road, where sweeping coastal vistas greet the determined hiker. Because of the heat and exposed terrain, as well as the stiff elevation gain, this trail is not recommended for travel during summer months. Spring brings fine wildflower displays and blooming yucca, and a clear blustery autumn day rewards the hiker with terrific views.

Although Jaime De Angulo posted signs on his property that read TRESPASSERS WELCOME, current residents of Partington Ridge are not so accommodating. The route passes near several residences. Respect private property.

Until the late 1980s, De Angulo Trail was a footpath that paralleled and crossed a private road; now the trail is the road itself for 1⅕ miles.

Directions to trailhead: Unsigned De Angulo Trail begins on the east side of Highway 1 at a turnout 8 miles south of Pfeiffer Big Sur State Park and about 1 mile south of Torre Canyon bridge.

The walk: Join the dirt road heading uphill from the parking turnout. It's a stiff, steady climb past rough driveways leading to residences. Enjoy the great views as you climb.

At 1⅕ miles you join a footpath traveling northward toward Torre Canyon. Ascending through tan-oak woodland and redwood forest, the trail reemerges onto sunbaked grassland and comes to a signed tractor trail. Follow this trail very briefly to another sign indicating that the trail leads upward. The trail climbs through grassland, past oak copses, and through a stand of pines atop the ridge separating Partington and Torre canyons.

Ascending through brush, the trail briefly intersects a steep, boulder-strewn firebreak and follows it upward. The trail leaves the firebreak and contours gently to the north to Coast Ridge Road. Superb views to the east and west and fine picnic spots reward the hiker.

Partington Cove

Partington Cove Trail

> **Terrain:** Hidden cove on dramatic Big Sur coastline.
> **Highlights:** Historic landing site; otter-watching.
> **Distance:** ½-mile round-trip.
> **Degree of difficulty:** Easy.

Partington Cove, part of Julia Pfeiffer Burns State Park, was once the site of a dock where tanbark was loaded onto waiting ships. During the 1880s, homesteader John Partington operated a landing here.

Woodsmen stripped the tanbark oak, a kind of cross between an oak and a chestnut. Before synthetic chemicals were invented to tan leather, gathering and shipping the bark was a considerable industry along the Big Sur coast.

This short leg-stretcher of a walk drops down to Partington Creek and over to the deep-blue waters of the cove.

Directions to trailhead: Partington Cove Trail begins 1⅕ miles north of the entrance to Julia Pfeiffer Burns State Park at the point where Highway 1 crosses Partington Creek.

The walk: From an iron gate, follow the dirt road that drops down into the canyon cut by Partington Creek. (A steep side trail continues down to the tiniest of beaches at the creek mouth.) The main trail crosses the creek on a wooden footbridge and passes through a hundred-foot-long tunnel that was blasted through the rocky cliffs.

At Partington Cove are the remains of a dock. The not-so-placid waters of the cove stir the seaweed about as if in a boiling soup, and you wonder how boats moored here actually managed to load their cargo of bark and lumber.

Offshore, between Partington Point and McWay Creek to the south, is Julia Pfeiffer Burns Underwater Area, placed under state protection in 1970. Kelp forests provide habitat for abalone, lingcod, and many more sea creatures, as well as for otters, which you may glimpse if you follow the crumbling cliffside trail from the dock site to the end of Partington Point.

Julia Pfeiffer Burns State Park
McWay Falls, Overlook Trails

> **Terrain:** Steep coastal bluffs.
> **Highlights:** Whale-watching, only major California waterfall on coast.
> **Distance:** ½- to ¾-mile each.
> **Degree of difficulty:** Easy.

For most visitors, Big Sur is synonymous with popular Pfeiffer Big Sur State Park. Often overlooked is a smaller slice of Big Sur located 10 miles south—Julia Pfeiffer Burns State Park.

It's a shame to overlook it. A redwood grove, dramatic coastal vistas, and the only major California waterfall to tumble into the Pacific are some of the park's attractions.

The park is a tribute to hardy pioneer Julia Pfeiffer Burns, remembered for her deep love of the Big Sur backcountry. Her father, Michael Pfeiffer, started a ranch in the Santa Lucia Mountains in 1869. In 1915 Julia Pfeiffer married John Burns, and the two ran a cattle ranch while living at their home located south of the present park.

During the 1920s, Lathrop Brown, a New York congressman and confidante to Franklin Roosevelt, and his wife, Helen, built Waterfall House on the bluffs above McWay Falls. Erected before the completion of Coast Highway, the isolated residence was surrounded by a lush garden of plants and flowers imported from around the world.

Easterner Helen Brown was an admirer of westerner Julia Pfeiffer Burns, and in 1962, more than three decades after her friend's death, she donated the Browns' property to the state. Helen Brown requested that Waterfall House become a park museum; however, the parks department insisted that it lacked sufficient funds to operate a museum and bulldozed the house into the sea.

You can easily sample the coastal charms of 4-square-mile Julia Pfeiffer Burns State Park by following the short Waterfall and Partington Cove Trail.

The park's coastal trails are great leg-stretcher jaunts to break up the coastal drive. They're particularly fine paths to hike in winter because they provide excellent observation points from which to sight migrating California gray whales.

Directions to trailhead: Julia Pfeiffer Burns State Park straddles Highway 1, 36 miles south of Carmel and 10 miles south of Pfeiffer Big Sur State Park. Turn inland into the park and proceed to the day-use lot.

The walk: From the Julia Pfeiffer Burns State Park lot, take the signed trail toward Scenic Overlook. Along McWay Creek you'll spot some eucalyptus, quite a botanical contrast to the redwoods growing upcreek. (In the spring, ceanothus and dogwood splash color along the trail.) The path leads through a tunnel under Coast Highway and emerges to offer the walker grand panoramas of the Big Sur coast.

You'll soon reach the overlook, where you can observe slender but dramatic McWay Falls tumbling 100 feet from the granite cliffs into McWay Cove.

On your return, you can take a side trail and meander over to the park's cypress-shaded environmental campsites, which are perched on the former site of Waterfall House.

Partington Canyon

Tanbark Trail

> **Terrain:** Redwood- and tan oak–forested canyon.
> **Highlights:** Lovely redwoods, historic Tin House.
> **Distance:** 7 miles round-trip with 2,000-foot elevation gain.
> **Degree of difficulty:** Moderate to strenuous.

Unlike McWay Canyon, neighboring Partington Canyon was spared the full wrath of the 1985 Rat Creek Fire; the redwoods, some of the most inspiring in Big Sur, remain.

A majority of the canyon's redwoods are second-growth. Partington, like most Big Sur canyons, was logged in the late nineteenth and early twentieth centuries. Keen-eyed hikers will spot notches in the downhill sides of redwood stumps; these notches held platforms upon which the sawyers stood while they cut.

The loggers who felled Partington's redwoods left behind virgin timber in the canyon's rugged upper reaches, along with some gnarled, crooked specimens that were apparently commercially ill-suited for lumber.

Tanoaks were harvested, too. The bark was stripped to make tannic acid, a chemical (before a synthetic substitute was invented) used to cure leather. Partington Cove (see related walk on page 100) was the shipping point for the products of these forest industries.

This walk travels through Partington Canyon to Tin House, supposedly built as a vacation retreat for the Lathrop Brown family. As the story goes, the considerable amount of tin used in the home's construction was salvaged from a closed gas station during World War II. Tin House has greatly deteriorated over the years but its inspiring view of the coastline remains.

Trail advocates are optimistic that a connector trail leading from Tanbark Trail to Ewoldsen Trail will one day be restored. This connection would offer a long and very satisfying hike through the Julia Pfeiffer Burns State Park backcountry.

Directions to trailhead: Tanbark Trail begins 1⅕ miles north of the Julia Pfeiffer Burns State Park entrance at the point where Highway 1 crosses Partington Creek. (This walk shares a trailhead with the Partington Cove walk.) The best parking is on the west side of the highway. Carefully cross the highway to the trailhead, located near the north side of the highway bridge.

The walk: Two minutes of walking brings tranquillity: tall redwoods, lush ferns, the lovely cascades of Partington Creek. Tanbark Trail crosses the creek on a footbridge. A short branch leads right back to the highway, while the main trail begins climbing the canyon wall on the south side of the creek.

The long ascent, which stays mostly in the redwood-tanoak forest, occasionally offers glimpses of the ocean and of one of Big Sur's "population centers"—some homes on Partington Ridge. The well-engineered path passes rock walls and bridge work built by Swedish homesteaders of the 1920s before making its way toward the ridge separating Partington and McWay canyons.

Before reaching the ridge crest, Tanbark Trail descends a bit to a junction with an old fire road that in turn leads to Tin House.

Partington Cove, one of Big Sur's tiny "doghole" ports.

Julia Pfeiffer Burns State Park

Ewoldsen Trail

> **Terrain:** Redwood forest, open grassland.
> **Highlights:** Some of Big Sur's largest redwoods; coastal vistas.
> **Distance:** 4³⁄₁₀-mile loop with 1,600-foot elevation gain.
> **Degree of difficulty:** Moderate to strenuous.

Sometimes visitors to Julia Pfeiffer Burns State Park are so enchanted by the spectacle of McWay Falls tumbling into the Pacific that they overlook the park's considerable backcountry—more than 3,600 acres of dramatic ridges, oak-dotted meadows, and rugged, redwood-filled canyons.

Ewoldsen Trail, named for the former ranch foreman who fashioned this path in 1933 from a onetime logging route, tours McWay Canyon and surrounding slopes. The trail was closed after the 1985 Rat Creek Fire burned most of the state park, but the lower portion has subsequently been repaired. Prefire Ewoldsen Trail connected to the Tanbark Trail; however, this upper length has not been reconstructed.

For the hiker, Ewoldsen Trail offers an intriguing contrast between the cool, quiet redwood groves in McWay Canyon and the exposed grassy coastal ridge. Fogless days mean splendid views from Lopez Point north to Pfeiffer Point.

Directions to trailhead: Julia Pfeiffer Burns State Park is located just off Highway 1, 36 miles south of Carmel and 10 miles south of Pfeiffer Big Sur State Park. Turn east into the park and proceed to the day-use lot.

The walk: Canyon Trail follows redwood-lined McWay Creek, passing the park's picnic area and crossing a bridge near an old barn. After ¼-mile, the path junctions. Canyon Trail continues a short distance up McWay Creek to reach a small waterfall.

Ewoldsen Trail switchbacks up the canyon wall amid a mixed forest of tanoak, bay laurel, and redwood. A bit more than a mile out, the trail reaches a junction. Fork right, taking the east leg of the Ewoldsen loop.

The path continues climbing along the cascading creek past fire-scarred redwoods. After ½-mile, the trail leaves McWay Canyon for scrubbier slopes, climbing ¾-mile to the ridge-top crest of the trail. Someday you'll be able to hike to Tin House and connect with Tanbark Trail, but for now, you'll continue your loop, following the path to a Pacific-facing grassland, then beginning a somewhat steep descent.

The coastal vistas are inspiring. This part of the trail is a good lookout perch for observing California gray whales during their winter migration. Less inspiring is the rather close-up view of the Great Slide of 1983—or rather the scar from its repair, a terraced wasteland that is still ugly despite extensive replanting efforts.

The trail departs the ridge, descending back into McWay Canyon and the tranquillity of its redwoods. You'll cross McWay Creek and close the loop, retracing your initial steps a mile back to the trailhead.

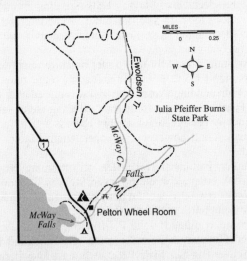

Pacific Valley

Pacific Valley Coast Trail

Terrain: Wide, flat marine terrace; sandy beach.
Highlights: Sand Dollar Beach, one of Big's Sur's best; great
bluff-top walking.
Distance: From Sand Dollar Picnic Area across bluffs is 2½
miles round-trip.
Degree of difficulty: Easy.

Near the hamlet of Pacific Valley, the Big Sur coast arcs deeply inland in a horseshoe shape that is fringed by a long sandy beach.
Sand Dollar Beach, one of Big Sur's longest sand strands, is a favorite of sunbathers and surfers; the wide bluffs above attract hikers as well as hang gliders looking for a safe landing spot.

Geologists say that Pacific Valley isn't really a valley at all but a
wide, flat marine terrace. (So precipitous are the Santa Lucia Mountains, early place-namers can be forgiven for calling any flatland
bigger than a blanket a valley.)

By whatever name, Pacific Valley is a marked contrast to most of
Big Sur's slopes, which tumble steeply and directly into the ocean.
The valley offers a rare bit of relatively level coast walking.

Crumbly schist and shale form the coastal terrace, which stands
60 to 100 feet above the surging Pacific. The bluff top is mostly
covered with grass, along with clumps of lizardtail, buckwheat, and
sagebrush.

The bluffs offer dramatic coastal views as well as providing a
good vantage point from which to spot sea otters and migrating
California gray whales. Cows are by far the most common animal
life here; Pacific Valley has been extensively grazed for decades.

You can join the trail from several hikers' stiles at Highway 1
turnouts located between Plaskett Creek Campground and the Pacific Valley store. The best place to start is at Sand Dollar Picnic
Area, where you have a choice of three coastal trails.

The main trail descends directly to Sand Dollar Beach. Pause en
route at the vista point, where interpretive panels help you identify
the many shorebirds found here.

From the northwest end of the parking area, a footpath travels the
cattle-grazed bluffs north of Sand Dollar Beach. The mile-long trail

dips in and out of two ravines and crosses what has to be one of the prettiest pastures on the Pacific coast. Shorter side trails lead to bluff-top overlooks and hidden pocket beaches.

A third path leads south ½-mile from Sand Dollar Picnic Area toward Jade Cove.

Directions to trailhead: The Forest Service's Sand Dollar Picnic Area is located west of Highway 1, 4 miles south of Mill Creek Picnic Area and about a mile south of the hamlet of Pacific Valley.

5. Big Sur Backcountry

Geographically, and some would say spiritually, Big Sur is the heart of California. The Big Sur backcountry is not a gentle wilderness but a dramatic, enchanted land, explored by more than 300 miles of trail.

What is popularly known as Big Sur is really the Santa Lucia Mountains, a range extending 90 miles from the Carmel Valley in the north to San Simeon in San Luis Obispo County. By far the most popular backcountry ports of entry are from Coast Highway. A less well known but nevertheless delightful journey into the wilderness can begin from the eastern entry points.

Trails probe the headwaters of the Arroyo Seco and the Little Sur and Big Sur rivers, which originate in the Ventana Wilderness. Observant hikers may spot the rare and beautiful Santa Lucia fir, a spirelike tree that grows only in the Santa Lucia Mountains. In these mountains also is the southernmost limit of the natural range of the redwood. Fern-lined canyons, oak-studded potreros, and meadows smothered with Douglas irises, pink owl's clover, and California poppies welcome the backcountry traveler.

Big Sur began receiving some measure of federal protection in 1906 when it became the Monterey National Forest. Today the land is under the jurisdiction of the Monterey District of Los Padres National Forest, as well as a handful of state parks. Much of the Forest Service land is kept in its primitive state as part of the 167,323-acre Ventana Wilderness.

In 1978 the Marble Cone Fire extensively damaged the Los Padres backcountry. Much of what was forest is now brushland and may not regain its timbered beauty for many more years. A number of steep timbered canyons and watersheds, however, escaped devastation. In many places Big Sur is as beautiful as ever, an attractive hiking destination for Southern Californians, Bay Area residents, and walkers from around the world.

Carmel River

Carmel River Trail

Terrain: Riparian woodland along banks of Carmel River.
Highlights: Wild (and sometimes wet) journey.
Distance: To Bluff Camp is 8⅗ miles round-trip with 200-foot
    elevation gain; to Carmel River Camp is 10 miles round-
    trip with 300-foot gain.
Degree of difficulty: Moderate.

Central Coast travelers know the Carmel River as the lazy stream making its mellow way to the Pacific just south of the town of Carmel. The upper reaches of the river, however, are a different Carmel—a wilderness watershed as wild as anywhere in the Big Sur backcountry.

A walk along the banks of the Carmel River can be delightful in any season. From December through March, the river is quite high, with some difficult crossings. Few hikers are willing to contend with the high water, so intrepid travelers are likely to have the river to themselves. (After a storm, river crossings are sometimes so dangerous that no hiker should tempt fate by fording the Carmel.)

Spring, with wildflowers abloom and the grasslands a deep green, is a fine time to hike the Carmel. The days are warm and the river can be forded by boulder-hopping.

Summer hikers delight in the shady canyon bottom and taking a plunge in the cool pools of the river. Autumn has its fans, too: days and evenings are a pleasant temperature, and the maples and sycamores wear their fall colors.

After contouring above the shores of Los Padres Reservoir, Carmel River Trail stays mostly by the river. You'll cross the river a couple of times on this hike to Carmel River Camp, but if you were to continue to Hiding Camp, you'd cross the river another two dozen times!

Directions to trailhead: From Highway 1 in Carmel, turn east on Carmel Valley Road (G–16) and drive 11½ miles to Carmel Valley village (best opportunity for gas and food), then another 4³⁄₁₀ miles to Cachagua Road. Turn right and follow this narrow road 6 miles to Nason Road. Turn right and drive ½-mile to a parking area and a gate across the road.

The walk: Near the road gate is a hiker/equestrian gate that you pass through to join the wide, oak-lined road. You'll cross a bridge over the dam's spillway, walk briefly by the dam, then turn south.

About 1½ miles from the trailhead, you'll pass a junction with a very steep road, a connector trail leading to a junction with the Big Pines Trail. In another ¼-mile, you'll reach a fork in the road and bear right on the fast-narrowing road that becomes Carmel River Trail. You'll soon pass the right-forking Big Pines Trail leading to Big Pines and Danish Creek.

Contouring over brushy slopes, Carmel River Trail travels high above Los Padres Reservoir. The path stays in the oak- and sycamore-shaded canyon for the most part except for a brief climb onto a chaparral-clad ridge and subsequent descent to shady Bluff Camp.

Boulder-hop across the creek. The path enters the Ventana Wilderness and ¾-mile from Bluff Camp passes a junction with Miller Canyon Trail. Keep right a short distance on Carmel River Trail to reach Carmel River Camp. Enjoy this oak-shaded retreat and the inviting nearby swimming holes.

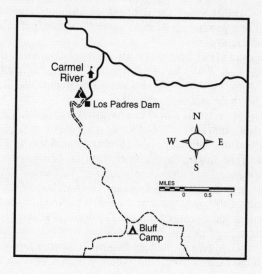

Mount Carmel

Skinner Ridge, Big Pines, Mount Carmel Trails

> **Terrain:** Mosaic of chaparral, oak, and madrone woodland.
> **Highlights:** Terrific 360-degree vistas of Monterey Bay and
> Big Sur; good weekend backpacking trip.
> **Distance:** From Bottcher's Gap to Skinner Ridge Viewpoint
> is 4¼ miles round-trip with 1,200-foot elevation gain; to
> Mount Carmel is 9½ miles round-trip with 2,300-foot ele-
> vation gain.
> **Degree of difficulty:** Moderate to strenuous.
> **Precautions:** Carry plenty of water—no reliable creeks or
> springs during summer months; ticks present in some
> brushy areas near trail.

Mount Carmel puts a lot of Big Sur at your feet. Three viewpoints
en route—Skinner Ridge, Devil's Peak, and Mount Carmel itself—
offer inspiring panoramas of what some California naturalists call
"the Middle Kingdom."

The majestic views from that northwestern landmark of the Ventana Wilderness, 4,417-foot-high Mount Carmel, include Carmel,
Salinas, Monterey Bay, and the Santa Cruz Mountains. The vistas
are well worth the strenuous day hike.

If you're interested in a weekend backpacking trip, the route over
Skinner Ridge into the Little Sur River watershed is ideal. From the
trailhead at Bottchers Gap, it's 10 miles round-trip to Comings
Camp. Madrone-shaded Pat Springs Camp, one of my favorite overnight destinations, is a round-trip sojourn of 14¼ miles.

During the summer months, hikers should check with rangers
about the availability of water at the area's backcountry campsites.
The spring at Pat Springs Camp is usually dependable, but other
creeks and springs can dry up by midsummer.

Bottchers Gap, where this hike begins, is a notch formed by the
Palo Colorado earthquake fault where it trends through a ridge.
These "gaps" occur elsewhere in the Santa Lucia Mountains where
faults cross ridges.

At Bottchers Gap is a campground and a parking area for day hikers. The trailhead, at 2,080 feet, gives hikers a nice head start for
the climb to come.

Directions to trailhead: From Highway 1 in Carmel, drive 12 miles south to the junction with Palo Colorado Road (this junction is ¼-mile south of the turnoff to Rocky Point Restaurant). Turn inland, climbing 7¾ miles to road's end at Bottcher's Gap Campground. Signed Skinner Ridge Trail begins at the northeast (upper-left) end of the camp's parking area.

The walk: The path ascends north, soon leaving behind the oak-shaded camp and heading into the chaparral. After brief exertion, hikers get the first of many views. To the northwest is the ocean; behind you, to the south, is the great white mountain Pico Blanco. Fortunately, conservationists have thus far saved this mountain of marble from the mining companies that would like to quarry it to smithereens.

The hike's second mile is viewless; the path zigzags, drops into gullies, and seems a bit disorienting at times. After crossing a field of bracken ferns, the trail makes a final short, but steep, climb to Skinner Ridge. Some of Big Sur's ecological complexity is apparent from the ridge: oak-dotted, golden grasslands; the light greens and grays of the chaparral on south-facing slopes; the dark greens of the hardwood forests on north-facing slopes.

A northward walk along the oak- and madrone-shaded ridge (some of the largest madrone on the central coast grow here) brings you to a saddle and a junction with Turner Creek Trail. This side trail leads to Apple Creek Trail Camp (½-mile) and to Turner Creek Trail Camp (1 mile). Both are pleasant overnight stops or picnic spots.

You continue on the main route—now known and sometimes signed as Big Pines Trail—for a steep, shadeless, and strenuous mile through ceanothus and manzanita to Devil's Peak viewpoint. The view includes the Pacific to the west, Pico Blanco to the south, and lonely Ventana Double Cone to the southeast.

Continue another ¹⁄₁₀-mile east to a junction with the left-bearing Mount Carmel Trail. You'll see a crude trail to the right that leads 50 yards to the actual summit of Devil's Peak, but as you'll soon observe, it's oak-covered and viewless, better for picnics than for panoramas.

March along a scrub oak–covered ridgeline ¾-mile to Mount Carmel's brushy, flat-topped summit. You wouldn't get much of a view from the top if it were not for the fortunate presence of a granite outcropping. Scramble up the chunk of granite, or the section of telephone pole that some considerate soul installed atop the peak, and marvel at the vista. Due north is Monterey and to the northwest is Pebble Beach and Carmel. On fogless days you can see Santa

Cruz, some 40 miles away, at the north end of Monterey Bay. To the northeast, about 20 miles away, is Salinas; to the west is the deep-blue Pacific; to the south, miles and miles of Big Sur backcountry.

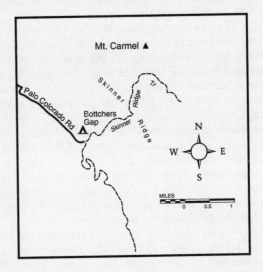

Pine Valley

Pine Ridge, Carmel River Trails

> **Terrain:** High, pine-ringed meadow.
> **Highlights:** Tall ponderosa pines, mellow meadowland; ideal weekend backpack.
> **Distance:** 13 miles round-trip with 1,500-foot elevation gain.
> **Degree of difficulty:** Moderate to strenuous.

Sandstone outcroppings and tall ponderosa pines increase the drama of one of the most scenic valleys in the Santa Lucias. Adding to the pastoral scene are the numerous deer who browse the valley and the woodpeckers who rat-a-tat-tat in the pines.

Pine Valley may appear to be all the more lovely because of its surroundings. The valley escaped the severe 1977 Marble Cone Fire while neighboring areas did not.

The valley is a truly fine day-hike destination, although most visitors are backpackers who enjoy the modest hike, mellow meadowland, and trail camp with dependable water source. It's accessible—and enjoyable—most of the year.

The elevated valley (3,150 feet) is situated above neighboring dark, damp, and cold canyons; its locale means that the valley is even an attractive winter destination—between rains, anyway. Summer days in the valley can be quite hot, but the ponderosas provide plenty of shade.

Directions to trailhead: From Highway 101 in Greenfield, exit onto Monterey County Road G–16 and head west 29 miles. Turn south on Tassajara Road and travel 1³⁄₁₀ miles to Cachagua Road. Turn left. After 1½ miles the road turns to dirt, continuing another 7½ miles to the trailhead just beyond the turnoff to China Campground, some 75 yards south of the camp's entrance road. Opposite the trailhead is parking for a half-dozen cars.

The walk: The path ascends ½-mile to a tanbark oak–dotted saddle. From atop the saddle are views (partially obscured by brush) of Cone Peak and other prominent Santa Lucia summits.

After a mile of dipping and climbing, the path begins a more steady descent through a ghostly forest of pines, oaks, and madrones scorched by the horrendous Marble Cone Fire. Amid the regenerating woodland are wide, grassy hillsides, from which hikers gain wilderness vistas.

Three and a half miles from the trailhead, you arrive at Church Creek Divide and a four-way junction. Church Creek Trail, the only one not of concern to the walker this day, heads southeast toward Church Creek, Pine Ridge Trail (your return route), and northwest-bound Carmel River Trail.

Carmel River Trail crosses the often dry headwaters of the Carmel River as it descends ½-mile to a (usually) more inspired watercourse. A scattering of Santa Lucia fir can be spotted near the riverside route, but it's the ponderosa pines that increasingly predominate as the trail approaches Pine Valley. Inspiring, too, are the commanding sandstone cliffs rising above the river.

The pines are numerous and the Carmel River is an all-year stream of some size by the time the hiker reaches Pine Valley Camp.

After sunbathing (or cooling off as the case might be), join the trail at the upper end of the camp. The path climbs steeply up a ridge, then continues along a ridgeline. At a saddle, ignore an abandoned connector trail descending to old Bear Basin Camp and instead continue climbing moderately with the main path southeast to its junction with Pine Ridge Trail. Retrace your steps 3½ miles back to the trailhead.

Ventana Wilderness Trails offer miles of solitary trails.

△ Manuel Peak

Manuel Peak Trail

Terrain: Steep Santa Lucia Mountains, oak forest, redwoods.
Highlights: One of Big Sur's best viewpoints.
Distance: From the state park to summit of Manuel Peak is
   10 miles round-trip with 3,100-foot elevation gain.
Degree of difficulty: Strenuous.

Arguably the best views of Big Sur can be found from the many au-tomobile turnouts along Coast Highway. These vista points offer glimpses of the region's dramatic cliffs and the tempestuous Pacific Ocean.

But if you want to see the whole of Big Sur—the Ventana Wilder-ness, the Santa Lucia Mountains, and the ocean that stretches, it seems, all the way to China—you have to take a hike. Such a broad panorama is the hiker's reward for reaching the summit of Manuel Peak.

Manuel Peak Trail climbs at a fairly steep—though not severe—gradient. More than half of the trail crosses exposed, chamise-clad slopes. The path is a bit brush-crowded in places but otherwise in good condition. The colder months (November–May) are best for the trek. No water is available en route.

Directions to trailhead: Make your way to Pfeiffer Big Sur State Park, just off Highway 1, some 65 miles north of Hearst Castle and 30 miles south of Carmel. A mile south of the state park is a helpful multiagency information center.

From the state park entrance station (day-use fee), drive past Big Sur Lodge and bear left on the park road leading to the picnic areas. At road's end you'll see the signed trail for Manuel Peak and other park trails.

The walk: Follow the park's paved service road for the five-minute walk to Homestead Cabin. Then join signed Oak Grove Trail, which ascends past oaks and over brushy slopes. A mellow ½-mile climb brings you to the signed junction with Manuel Peak Trail.

Bear right and tackle 6 switchbacks that climb coastal scrub–dotted slopes. The reward for this steep bit of zigging and zagging is your first coastal view.

Even more compelling, as you climb east, is the sight and (in the wet season) the thunderous sound of the Big Sur River.

About 3 miles from the trailhead, the path heads into a mixed forest of live oaks and madrone, tanbark oak and redwood.

Leaving the forest behind, you resume ascending brushy slopes for another ¼-mile to a ravine watered by a seasonal creek. Just past the creek crossing, a short side trail leads a few paces to a spring.

Now you contour around dry slopes, getting yucca-framed views of the coast to the southwest and the Big Sur landmark Ventana Double Cone to the northeast.

After climbing past chaparral and through oak woodland, you emerge onto a ridge that offers coastal views. Ahead is a white reflector that marks Manuel Peak's viewpoint.

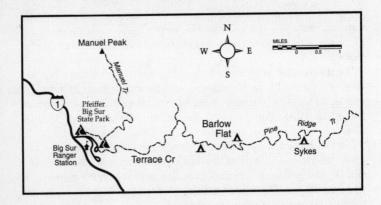

Sykes Hot Springs

Pine Ridge Trail

Terrain: Steep, redwood-shaded slopes and canyons.
Highlights: Beautiful trail through heart of Big Sur; a hot springs welcomes hardy hikers.
Distance: To Ventana Camp Junction is 4¼ miles one way with 1,100-foot elevation gain; to Barlow Flat is 7 miles; to Sykes Camp is 10 miles; to Redwood Creek Camp is 12 miles with 1,400-foot elevation gain.
Degree of difficulty: Moderate to strenuous.

Sykes Camp, on the banks of the Big Sur River, has a little bit of everything—morning sun, afternoon shade, a deep swimming hole, and hot springs. The camp is a 10-mile journey from Pfeiffer Big Sur State Park, and one of California's classic weekend backpacking trips.

Sykes's charms are undeniable, but seekers of solitude should steer clear on weekends during the summer months. Rangers estimate that in some years about 75 percent of the backcountry use in the Monterey District of Los Padres National Forest occurs along the 10 miles of trail from Pfeiffer Big Sur State Park to Sykes.

If you like to swim, Ventana Camp has some excellent swimming holes. It's a 10-mile round-trip day hike to reach the camp.

Directions to trailhead: Pfeiffer Big Sur State Park is about 26 miles south of Carmel on Highway 1. The trailhead for Pine Ridge Trail is located about a mile south of the park entrance at a wide turnout on the east side of the highway. Close by is the Big Sur Multi-Agency Facility—an information center.

The walk: Leaving the highway behind, Pine Ridge Trail marches up redwood-shaded slopes above Big Sur Campground. Manuel Peak dominates the northern skyline, while the Pacific can be glimpsed behind you.

The trail passes through a tanbark-oak forest, enters the Ventana Wilderness, and offers westward views of the Big Sur River. After about 4 miles of dipping and climbing, you'll reach a junction with a side trail leading to Ventana Camp, 1¼ miles north. For a walk of slightly more than 10 miles round-trip, take the trail to Ventana Camp, located near the convergence of Ventana Creek and the Big

Sur River. In 1968 the camp achieved national notoriety when the U.S. Forest Service closed it for a time owing to the so-called hippie problem. Near the camp is a great swimming hole. After lunch and a swim, return to the trailhead.

Pine Ridge Trail continues east for a mile to another side trail. This one leads a short distance to redwood-shaded Terrace Creek Camp, another destination that would make an ideal lunch stop and turnaround point for a day hike.

Pine Ridge Trail crosses Terrace Creek, ascends through woodland, descends a hill, crosses Logwood Creek, and arrives at Barlow Flat. This flat, expansive camp is on the north side of the Big Sur River in the shade of redwoods. It's a great location for swimming and sunbathing. Leaving Barlow Flat, the trail stays below the river for another 3 miles until it reaches Sykes Camp.

A ¼-mile downriver is Sykes Hot Springs, reached by some wading and a side trail. The site includes a couple of hot seeps dammed to create small pools, as well as a big 10-foot-long, rock-lined pool. You'll enjoy basking in the 100°F waters and gazing at the night sky.

Two more miles of steep, uphill travel on Pine Ridge Trail will bring you to Redwood Creek Camp, which has several tent sites. It's a rarely visited alternative to Sykes Camp.

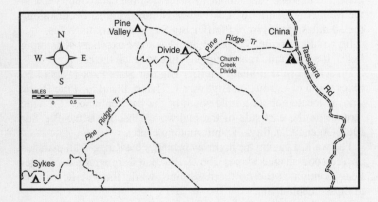

Arroyo Seco

Arroyo Seco Trail

Terrain: Headwaters of Arroyo Seco, lush riparian environment.

Highlights: Pools, pleasant creekside journey, good vistas from Coast Ridge.

Distance: To Forks Camp is 3½ miles round-trip with elevation gain; to Madrone Camp is 6 miles round-trip with 1,000-foot elevation gain; to Coast Ridge is 10 miles round-trip with 2,000-foot gain.

Degree of difficulty: Moderate to strenuous.

Don't be put off by the name. Arroyo Seco (Spanish for "Dry Creek") is anything but seco near its headwaters. Cascades, tiny waterfalls, and inviting pools are some of the aquatic charms of the upper Arroyo Seco, which spills down a sometimes narrow, sometimes wide channel through the Ventana Wilderness.

The Arroyo Seco is a better-known destination downstream at Arroyo Seco Campground, where a developed campground, picnic areas, and swimming holes are popular with visitors—particularly Salinas Valley residents who flock there to escape the broiling Central Valley summers.

Few visitors, however, hike the upper watershed of the Arroyo Seco, which offers some of Big Sur's most intriguing backcountry. In the creek itself are many large sandstone boulders, diverting the waters into numerous pools and cascades.

Oak, sycamore, maple, and cottonwood are part of Arroyo Seco's lush riparian woodland, along with a scattering of incense cedar and the rare Santa Lucia fir. Crowding the creek in places are willows, ferns, blackberry bushes, and plenty of poison oak.

Arroyo Seco Trail is a moderately graded ascent along the creek to Forks and Madrone camps; beyond, the path climbs to the coastal crest of the Santa Lucia Mountains for excellent wilderness vistas.

Directions to trailhead: From Highway 101, some 30 miles south of King City, exit on Jolon Road (Monterey County Road G–18) and follow it 16 miles to the hamlet of Jolon. Turn right (north) on Jolon Road, soon stopping at the Fort Hunter Liggett entrance kiosk to check in, then continuing 5½ miles to a junction with Del Ventura Road. Mission San Antonio de Padua is straight ahead, but you swing left, continuing to Milpitas Road, entering national forest land, and proceeding 17½ miles to the end of the paved road at Santa Lucia Memorial Park Campground. Continue past the camp to a road fork. Park near the fork.

The walk: Follow the gated road on the left some 200 yards to cabins belonging to the Southern Monterey Sportsmen Association and the beginning of Arroyo Seco Trail. The path passes handsome sandstone formations known as The Rocks and travels ¼-mile to the Arroyo Seco. The creek here is sometimes deep and swift so use caution when you cross.

After another 1½ miles, the trail reaches oak-shaded Forks Camp. Two hundred yards beyond the camp, the trail forks. To the right, Rodeo Flat Trail (really a ridiculously steep, waterless, shadeless firebreak) ascends toward North Coast Ridge Trail.

Arroyo Seco Trail angles left, recrosses Arroyo Seco, climbs a bit more, then crosses Arroyo Seco again. Three miles from the trailhead is Madrone Camp, which boasts all-year water. From here, the path ascends through an area slowly recovering from the 1977 Marble Cone Fire. You get views behind you of the Arroyo Seco as well as Junipero Serra Peak, the highest summit of the Santa Lucias.

For a time, the path follows a line of burned World War II–era telephone poles, then reaches a junction with Cone Peak Trail at a

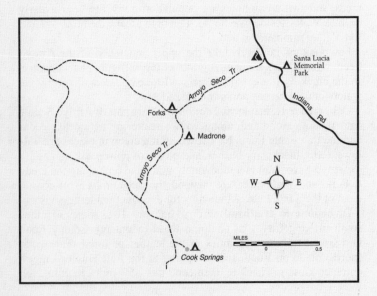

saddle 5 miles from the trailhead. Head northwest a short distance to enjoy the coastward and inland views. You can also walk southeast a mile along viewful Cone Peak Trail to a junction with Cook Springs Camp Trail, an abandoned road that descends a short, steep ½-mile to the pine-shaded camp.

Lost Valley

Lost Valley Trail

Terrain: Mellow grassland fringed with Coulter pine.
Highlights: Pleasant valley, one of Big Sur's best backcountry camps.
Distance: From Escondido Camp to Lost Valley Camp is 11 miles round-trip with 700-foot elevation gain.
Degree of difficulty: Moderate to strenuous.
Precautions: Rainy season road closure at Santa Lucia Memorial Camp.

A wide meadow spiked with Coulter pine is one reason hikers go out of their way to find Lost Valley. Experienced backpackers rank Lost Valley Camp as one of the top-three Ventana Wilderness campsites (along with Vicente Flat and Pine Valley).

Lost Valley is all the more precious because its pines and pastoral beauty were spared the wrath of the 1977 Marble Cone Fire that incinerated much of the surrounding wilderness.

The fault-formed valley is drained by Lost Valley Creek to the southeast and Higgins Creek to the northwest. The two creeks join forces and flow east toward the Arroyo Seco. The lower reaches of Lost Valley Creek are havens for wildlife: wood ducks, mallards, belted kingfishers, and Western pond turtles.

For the day hiker, "Why go?" is a far easier question to answer than "When to go?"

Springtime (wildflowers abound March through May) is a terrific season for hiking to Lost Valley. The trouble is, the Forest Service closes the last 3 miles of road to Escondido Campground during the rainy season—meaning that a comfortable 11-mile day hike becomes a 17-mile trek. On the bright side, if you walk the extra miles, you'll likely have the flower show, the emerald green grassland, and Lost Valley all to yourself.

Directions to trailhead: From Highway 101, some 30 miles south of King City, exit on Jolon Road (Monterey County Road G–18) and follow it 16 miles to the hamlet of Jolon. Turn right (north) on Jolon Road, soon stopping at the Fort Hunter Liggett entrance kiosk to check in, then continuing 5½ miles to a junction with Del Ventura Road. Mission San Antonio de Padua is straight ahead, but you swing left toward Milpitas Road, entering national forest land and continuing to Santa Lucia Memorial Park Campground. When the road is closed during the rainy months, the hike begins here. Otherwise, continue another 3 miles to Escondido Campground and the trailhead at the far end of the camp road.

The walk: From the campground, the path descends moderately a mile down brushy slopes to the Arroyo Seco. Ford the wide, boulder-strewn river, then begin a stiff, 1½-mile climb to a saddle. Enjoy the wilderness views, dominated by nearby Junipero Serra Peak, then begin a mellow descent toward Lost Valley Creek.

Four miles from the trailhead, the path crosses the creek to Fish Camp, then ascends ¾-mile to a minor divide and a junction with Lost Valley Connector, a firebreak trail. You stay with Lost Valley Trail, descending northwest to Lost Valley Creek and the Coulter pine–shaded trail camp located ½-mile from the divide.

Lost Valley Trail offers many options.

Junipero Serra Peak

Santa Lucia Trail

> **Terrain:** Tallest Santa Lucia Mountains peak.
> **Highlights:** Panoramic vistas of Ventana Wilderness and beyond.
> **Distance:** From Indians Station to summit is 12 miles round-trip with 3,700-foot elevation gain.
> **Degree of difficulty:** Strenuous.

It's the biggest mountain of Big Sur and it offers one of the grandest vistas. Panoramic views from atop 5,862-foot Junipero Serra Peak are splendid: much of the Ventana Wilderness, 60 miles of Pacific Ocean, slivers of the Salinas Valley, and the Sierra crest in Kings Canyon National Park.

The mountain supports rare plants such as the Santa Lucia lupine and Santa Lucia bedstraw, as well as stands of pine and hardwood forest recovering from the devastating Marble Cone Fire. Slopes once forested with sugar pines are now blanketed by brush. Still, the nature lover will find satisfaction in stands of Coulter pine, blue-oak woodland, and such spring-bloomers as monkey flower, manzanita, and woolly blue curls.

The mountain is named for one of early California's well-known Spanish missionaries, Father Junípero Serra. The mission nearest to the peak is San Antonio de Padua, founded in 1771 and today situated within the boundaries of Fort Hunter Liggett Military Reservation. Mission San Antonio (and many other California missions) "landscaped" its grounds with giant prickly pear cacti, brought by the padres from Mexico. Often called mission cactus, it can be seen at many of the missions, as well as in clusters near the beginning of the Junipero Serra Peak Trail.

The path to the peak is a moderately steep, mostly shadeless, unrelenting ascent. Your goal—the abandoned fire lookout tower atop the peak—is visible from the trailhead.

The best vistas from the peak are during the rainy season, late autumn to midspring.

Directions to trailhead: From Highway 101, some 30 miles south of King City, exit on Jolon Road (Monterey County Road G–18) and follow it 16 miles to the hamlet of Jolon. Turn right (north) on

Jolon Road, soon stopping at the Fort Hunter Liggett entrance kiosk to check in, then continuing 5½ miles to a junction with Del Ventura Road. Mission San Antonio de Padua is straight ahead, but you swing left, continuing to Milpitas Road, entering national forest land, and proceeding 17½ miles to Santa Lucia Memorial Park Campground.

The walk: The path passes the grasslands of Santa Lucia Memorial Park. Nearby are handsome sandstone formations, eroded into some intriguing configurations. A mile out, you crest a minor saddle, which offers a taste of the grand views to come. The path travels through an arroyo and some brushland before reaching a saddle halfway to the summit.

Your climb is eased a bit by some well-graded switchbacks. Another 1½ miles of ascent past a charred woodland brings you to another saddle. The path angles east, traversing past sugar pine and Coulter pine.

Eventually the trail turns south, ending on the west side of the peak near the abandoned lookout tower.

Among the wilderness peaks at your feet are Cone Peak, Ventana Double Cone, and Uncle Sam Mountain.

Cone Peak

Cone Peak Trail

Terrain: Steepest coastal slope in the continental United States.
Highlights: Ecologically unique mountain, glorious views of the Santa Lucia Mountains.
Distance: To Cone Peak summit is 4½ miles round-trip with 1,400-foot elevation gain.
Degree of difficulty: Moderate to strenuous.

Cone Peak, a geographical landmark to coast travelers for more than a hundred years, is the most abrupt pitch of country along the Pacific coast. It rises from sea level to 5,155 feet in about 3½ miles. On a clear day in winter, as you stand on Sand Dollar Beach, the snow-covered peak is a stirring sight.

Botanically, Cone Peak is a very important mountain. On its steep slopes Thomas Coulter and David Douglas discovered the Santa Lucia fir, considered the rarest fir in North America. (Tree lovers know that when names were attached to western cone-bearing trees, Coulter's went to a pine and Douglas's to a fir.)

The spirelike Santa Lucia fir, or bristlecone fir, is found only in scattered stands in northern San Luis Obispo and southern Monterey counties in the Santa Lucia Mountains. Typically, this fir occurs above the highest coast redwoods within mixed evergreen forest. Santa Lucia fir concentrates in steep, rocky, fire-resistant spots at elevations of 2,000 to 5,000 feet.

The precipitous trail to the top of Cone Peak rewards the hiker with great Big Sur views. Cone Peak's steepness contributes to its habitat diversity—apparent to toiling hikers who work their way slowly up the mountain's pine- and fir-dotted slopes.

Directions to trailhead: From Highway 1, 4 miles south of Lucia and just south of Kirk Creek Campground, or about 9 miles north of Gorda, turn east on Nacimiento Road. This road provides dramatic coastal views as it ascends sharply 7 miles to Nacimiento Summit. At the signed junction at the summit, turn left on graded Cone Peak Road and follow it 5 miles north along the ridge to the signed trail junction on the west side of the road. Parking is adequate for a few cars. (*Warning:* During the rainy season, Cone Peak Road may be closed.)

The walk: The well-graded trail crosses brush-covered slopes and soon begins a series of steep switchbacks. You'll enjoy views of Santa Lucia fir and Coulter pine. As the trail gains elevation, sugar pine predominates.

After gaining more than 2,000 feet in 2 miles, hikers reach a signed junction. (A trail leads west 1¼ miles down to steep, deeply shaded Trail Springs Camp. For an interesting loop around Cone Peak, you can join Gamboa Trail and ascend another 1¼ miles to the Cone Peak Trail. You can then follow Cone Peak Trail to its junction with Coast Ridge Road [Cone Peak Road] and proceed a mile back down the road to your vehicle.)

From this junction, the Cone Peak summit trail ascends a final ¼-mile eastward to the fire lookout atop Cone Peak. The lookout is staffed during the fire season.

Enjoy fine views of the valleys to the east and the coastline to the west. Spread before you is a panorama of peaks: Pinyon Peak, Ventana Double Cone, Junipero Serra Peak, Uncle Sam Mountain.

Return the same way, or hike the optional loop through Trail Springs Camp and around the great peak.

▲

Vicente Flat

Kirk Creek Trail

Terrain: Redwood-lined canyons, open grassy slopes.
Highlights: Mellow Vicente Flat, good coastal views.
Distance: From Coast Highway to Espinosa Camp is 6½
    miles round-trip with 1,400-foot elevation gain; to Vicente
    Campground is 10 miles round-trip with 2,000-foot gain.
Degree of difficulty: Moderate.

Kirk Creek Trail (often called Vicente Flat Trail) provides an ideal
introduction to the charms of Big Sur, for in 5 miles the walker ex-
periences meadowland, coastal and canyon views, and a redwood
forest.

Kirk Creek Trail climbs from coastal scrub–covered slopes to
redwood-shaded ravines to steep ridges offering dramatic vistas.
Vicente Flat, which boasts campsites in both shady redwoods and
sunny meadow, is a rewarding and relaxing destination.

You can make this a one-way hike if car-shuttle arrangements are
made. Join the upper trailhead for 7-mile Kirk Creek Trail at Cone
Peak Road (also called Coast Ridge Road) and hike 2 miles to Vicente Flat, then 5 miles down to Highway 1.

Directions to trailhead: The signed trail is located opposite Kirk
Creek Campground on Highway 1, just north of the Nacimiento
Road turnoff.

The walk: The trail immediately begins ascending on a series of
well-graded switchbacks through brush and grassland. Sweeping
views of the coast from Jade Cove to Gamboa Point are yours. One
nice feature of this walk is the way it alternates from sunny exposed
slopes to shady redwood ravines.

Three miles along, after topping a ridge, you'll reach the high
point of Vicente Flat Trail and enjoy fine coastal views. Next you'll
begin contouring above the watershed of Hare Canyon.

Tiny Espinosa Camp is 3¼ miles from the trailhead. Water is another ¼-mile uptrail, where a tiny unnamed creek cascades down a
redwood-lined ravine to the trail.

The trail ascends briefly, then makes a short descent to Hare Creek
and follows it. After crossing the creek, the walker encounters signed

Stone Ridge Trail junction, located on a low rise above the creek. To reach Vicente Flat Campground, hike upstream 150 yards.

Redwoods shade idyllic campsites. Water usually flows, even in summer, and a lovely meadow beckons picnickers and sun worshipers.

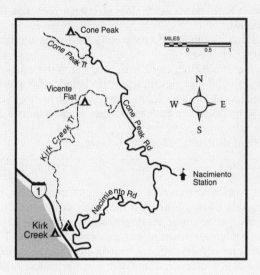

Silver Peak Wilderness

Salmon Creek Trail

Terrain: Steep Santa Lucia slopes, fern canyons, oak-dotted meadows.

Highlights: Southernmost redwood grove, magnificent views of Big Sur coast.

Distance: From Highway 1 to Spruce Camp is 4 miles round-trip with 800-foot elevation gain; to Estrella Camp is 6½ miles round-trip with 1,200-foot gain; return via Cruick-shank and Buckeye trails is 14 miles round-trip with 3,000-foot gain.

Degree of difficulty: Moderate to strenuous.

In the far southwestern corner of Monterey County, near the border with San Luis Obispo County, is the newly designated Silver Peak Wilderness. The area was geographically gerrymandered out of the Ventana Wilderness when it was established in 1984. The Sierra Club and other conservationists periodically mounted campaigns to add wilderness protection to the area and were successful in 1992 when Congress established the 14,500-acre Silver Peak Wilderness.

This little-visited wilderness at the far southern end of the Los Padres National Forest's Monterey District is home to an isolated grove of coastal redwoods along Villa Creek; it's the world's southernmost stand. Other botanical highlights include a grove of rare Sargent cypress at the head of Salmon Creek. The gray pine and Santa Lucia fir that bristle atop the peaks and the files of oaks growing in the mountains' folds and hollows are delights for photographers.

Three frisky creeks flow from the mountains to the sea: Villa Creek, Salmon Creek, and San Carpojo Creek. Hikers may see deer, squirrels, rabbits, and raccoons, as well as those trailside sunbathers—lizards. If you hear something gobble in the bushes, it's no doubt the call of a native wild turkey.

This hike, suitable for a strenuous day trip or more leisurely weekend backpack, offers a chance to sample the diversity of the south end of the Santa Lucia Mountains—lush fern canyons, fir forests, oak pasturelands—and sweeping views of the majestic coast and Salinas Valley.

Directions to trailhead: Salmon Creek Ranger Station (closed, but a good landmark) is located on Coast Highway a few miles north of the San Luis Obispo–Monterey county line. The trailhead is 100 yards south of the station.

Note the trailhead for Buckeye Trail located above the station. Buckeye Trail is your return path on your Silver Peak Wilderness loop.

Ample parking is available at the station. Signed Salmon Creek Trail begins on the east side of the highway on the south side of the creek. At the beginning of the trail, there's a great view of Salmon Creek Falls.

The walk: Salmon Creek Trail immediately begins climbing, first through lush streamside vegetation, then across the exposed slopes of the canyon, covered with seasonal wildflowers. The often dense fog here guards the flower show late into spring.

A thousand feet above sea level, the trail crosses a stream and ascends into a forest of Douglas fir, often called spruce—which helps explain the forthcoming destinations of Spruce Creek and Spruce Camp.

Two miles from the trailhead is the Spruce Creek Trail junction. The trail to the right leads south toward Dutra Spring and San Carpojo Creek. The main trail continues straight ahead up the main canyon of Salmon Creek. A few hundred yards of walking and you'll drop down to Spruce Creek Camp, located at the confluence of the waters of Salmon and Spruce creeks. Spruce Creek Camp is in deep shade.

The trail resumes on the other side of Spruce Creek and continues along the south slope of Salmon Creek. You cross a meadow, then continue ascending moderately to Estrella Camp, a grassy, shady area along Salmon Creek.

The trail soon rises above the last trees and ventures out onto hot, brushy canyon slopes. You climb 1,800 feet in the next 2½ miles; this is a very hot stretch of trail in summer.

You reach the high point of the trail (3,120 feet) at Coast Ridge Road, which marks the boundary between Fort Hunter Liggett Military Reservation and Los Padres National Forest. Bear left on the road. On clear days you'll be able to see the ocean to the west and the Salinas Valley to the east. In ¹⁄₁₀-mile, you'll reach the junction with Cruickshank Trail. Descend ½-mile on a rough, eroded road to Lion Den Camp—two small, flat areas, often situated just above the coastal clouds. The water supply is from a small creek.

Leaving Lion Den, you follow Silver Peak Road ½-mile to a junction. (Peak-baggers won't overlook 3,950-foot Silver Peak on the left.) Cross the road and follow the Cruickshank Trail. The trail descends, crossing a creek, and drops 1,000 feet in the next 2½ miles. You'll get fine views of the Villa Creek drainage. In spring, waterfalls can be seen cascading down the canyon. Silver Camp, not shown on forest service maps, is a streamside camp with plenty of flat tenting sites.

Three-quarters of a mile from Silver Camp, you veer south on the Buckeye Trail at Cruickshank Camp. The path begins ascending through heavy timber, climbing the shady north slope. The trail descends to Redwood Creek, crosses it, and proceeds south along the ridge separating Villa Creek and Redwood Creek canyons. The trail grows more tentative as it enters a meadow and reaches Buckeye Camp, which has a developed spring.

Leaving the meadowland, you contour around to the western slopes, receiving the twin pleasures of ocean breezes and coastal views. You descend a ridge, cross Soda Springs Creek, and arrive at a signed junction. Buckeye Trail (signed Soda Springs Trail) leads to Highway 1. This hike heads south, descending a mile through grassland and chaparral back to the trailhead (behind the Salmon Creek Ranger Station).

6. Southern Santa Lucia Mountains

Extending northwest to southeast, a series of mountain ranges roughly parallels the San Luis Obispo County coastline. These mountains include the southern Santa Lucias, as well as more inland summits such as the La Panza Range east of Santa Margarita.

Beginning north of Highway 41 between Atascadero and Morro Bay, the southern Santa Lucia Mountains extend to the Cuyama River on the border with Santa Barbara County. Some 190,000 acres of this steep mountain country are under the jurisdiction of Los Padres National Forest.

While the Monterey District (Big Sur backcountry) and the Santa Lucia District of Los Padres are about the same size, the northern Santa Lucias receive many, many times more visitors. In part, this is because Big Sur draws travelers from around the world and because the bulk of the backcountry is preserved in Ventana Wilderness and blessed with hundreds of miles of trail.

The southern Santa Lucias are unknown to most travelers and can boast of few good trails. In addition, access to the southern Santa Lucias is difficult because much private property lies between the natural features and public roads.

The centerpiece of the southern Santa Lucias is the 21,678-acre Santa Lucia Wilderness. Hikers head for the Lopez, Big Falls, and Little Falls canyons. Another highlight is Cerro Alto, which means "high (or difficult) mountain" in Spanish. The 2,620-foot mountain, located along West Cuesta Ridge, is high enough to offer grand coastal views from San Simeon to Point Sal.

Lake San Antonio

Nature, Harris Creek, Basham Point Trails

> **Terrain:** Lakeshore, oak-dotted hills.
> **Highlights:** Leg-stretcher of a hike halfway between Los Angeles and San Francisco.
> **Distance:** 1 to 5 miles round-trip.
> **Degree of difficulty:** Easy to moderate.

Lake San Antonio is located, a park brochure claims, "in the Central Coast area of California."

Well, maybe.

The lake's geographical position near the backside of Big Sur gives it some claim to Central Coast fame. So does its location within the boundaries of one of California's best-known coastal counties—Monterey. Cool winters and the spring wildflower display in San Antonio Valley also bolster the lake's Central Coast status.

But other scenes and seasons argue that Lake San Antonio is more a part of the Central Valley than the Central Coast. Near the lake, agriculture abounds—rolling grasslands dotted with cattle, miles of manicured orchards, grainfields, and almond groves. And the lake itself, Monterey County's largest, is a reservoir created in the late 1950s for use by Salinas Valley farmers and ranchers.

The lake's dual personality also extends to its recreational opportunities. In summer, when temperatures regularly reach the nineties, waterskiing, jet skiing, swimming, and sunbathing are favorite activities—and typical of the great Central Valley's huge "reservoir parks." During cooler months, the lake is a tranquil place, ideal for camping, bird-watching, and hiking.

Rangers advise a hike during the quiet months, November to May. Autumn is fine hiking weather; in winter you can go out on the lake with a bald eagle boat tour; and the spring wildflower bloom is highlighted by the park's annual Wildflower Festival during the first weekend of May.

Eagle Watch Boat Tours are scheduled from December through March on Fridays, Saturdays, and Sundays. Call the park for more information.

The park has some 20 miles of trails—footpaths, rough fire roads, and hillside fuel breaks. A 1-mile nature trail loop, complete with an interpretive brochure, introduces hikers to local flora and geology. Harris Creek Trail (¾-mile one way) leads along the lakeshore from Harris Creek Campground to the park's most inviting beach.

The best hike in the park is along Basham Point Trail, which begins at road's end at Basham Point on the Harris Creek arm of the lake. The path (2½ miles one way) leads west along Harris Creek, a sometimes spooky-looking watercourse when morning mists linger over ghostly, half-submerged oak trees. When the trail reaches a park boundary fence (cows graze the private hills beyond), it swings sharply right (north) and ascends an oak-lined draw to Redonda Vista Campground.

Directions to trailhead: Getting to the lake, located about halfway between Los Angeles and San Francisco, can be half the fun. (A stop at Lake San Antonio is a good way to break up the Southern California to Bay Area drive.) One good way to go is by leaving Highway 101 just north of Paso Robles on G–14 (Lake Drive). Head north past almond orchards and rolling blue oak–dotted hills. Stay with G–14 as it assumes two more identities (Nacimiento Lake Drive and Interlake Road) and winds between Lake Nacimiento and Lake San Antonio. Turn east on San Antonio Road and follow it a few miles to the park.

Cerro Alto

Cerro Alto Trail

> **Terrain:** Rugged, chaparral-covered slopes.
> **Highlights:** Coast and Coast Range panoramas.
> **Distance:** From campground to Cerro Alto Peak is 4 miles round-trip with 1,600-foot elevation gain; optional return route totals 5¾ miles round-trip. (If the campground road is closed, add another 1¾ miles to the round-trip.)
> **Degree of difficulty:** Moderate to strenuous.

At 2,620 feet, Cerro Alto ("high, or difficult, mountain") is certainly high enough to offer grand coastal views from San Simeon to Point Sal.

The serious Highway 41 Fire of August 1994 scorched West Cuesta Ridge, including the slopes of Cerro Alto. For a long time thereafter, signs along the highway offered a $100,000 reward for information leading to the arrest of the arsonist who started this blaze.

While it will be many years before the vegetation on Cerro Alto fully recovers from the fire, the main attraction of Cerro Alto Trail—the splendid view—remains unaltered; in fact, uncrowded by brush, postfire vistas may even have improved. Hikers can take solace in the mountain's spring wildflower display, particularly fields of California poppies.

Erosion from winter rains following the fire wiped out one spur of the campground road and the camp's water system; it may be a couple of years before the Forest Service repairs Cerro Alto. Until the camp is reopened, you'll need to walk about 9/10-mile up paved Forest Service Road.

Most of Cerro Alto Trail is unshaded, as it was even before the fire, so get an early start. If your party is seeking a pleasant family walk rather than a summit climb, I suggest the 2½-mile loop on the slopes above the campground.

Directions to trailhead: From Highway 101 in Atascadero, take the Highway 41 exit and head west 8 miles to the turnoff for the Cerro Alto Campground on the south side of the highway. From Highway 1 just north of Morro Bay, turn east on Highway 41 and drive 7½ miles to the campground turnoff.

If Cerro Alto Camp is open, drive %10-mile up the paved Forest Service road and park in the campground. If the road is closed to vehicles, leave your car by the information boards and walk up the road.

The more obvious trailhead, signed "Cerro Alto Trail," is at the far end of the campground beyond the traffic turnaround; however, this walk begins a bit lower at the wooden footbridge leading over Morro Creek.

The walk: Cross Morro Creek on the bridge. The path first meanders through a seared but unbowed live-oak woodland, then climbs steeper, chaparral-covered slopes. Three-quarters of a mile from the trailhead is a junction with a jeep road. Turn left, walking 200 yards to a junction with the summit trail. The old road (your optional return route) contours west, but Cerro Alto Trail begins a steep climb.

At ¼-mile farther, you'll pass a toasted grove of oak and bay, then continue another ½-mile to some switchbacks and views of Cambria and Morro Bay.

At ¼-mile from the summit, the trail reaches a junction with a road. Turn left and circle the summit as you ascend. From the summit, enjoy clear-day views of Piedras Blancas Light Station north of San Simeon, and perhaps as far south down the coast as Point Sal in Santa Barbara County. To the northeast is the city of Atascadero; farther east, the austere Temblor Range.

Back at the junction with the old jeep road, you can turn right if you wish to take a different route back. The road passes some burned-out bay trees, and farther on, some blacked madrone. The road leads to a trail, which descends the drainage of upper Morro Creek to Cerro Alto Campground.

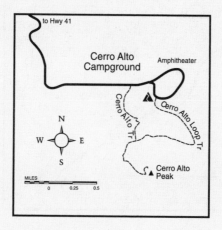

Little Falls

Little Falls Trail

Terrain: Wooded canyon.
Highlights: Waterfall, numerous pools.
Distance: To Little Falls is 1 mile round-trip; to Hi Mountain
Road is 5½ miles round-trip with 1,350-foot elevation gain.
Degree of difficulty: Easy to moderate.

Little Falls, little only in comparison to neighboring Big Falls, tumbles a more-than-respectable 50 feet into a pool. Above the falls are several more water-sculpted pools, perfect for wading or cooling off on a hot summer's day.

Little Falls Canyon is lushly vegetated with oak, sycamore, maple, and bay. From the upper reaches of the canyon are inspiring views of the Santa Lucia Wilderness.

For hikers looking for a longer sojourn, I recommend making a 12-mile loop by way of Little Falls Trail, Hi Mountain Road, Big Falls Trail, and Lopez Canyon Road.

Directions to trailhead: From Highway 101 in Arroyo Grande, take the Lopez Lake exit and head east on Highway 227, following

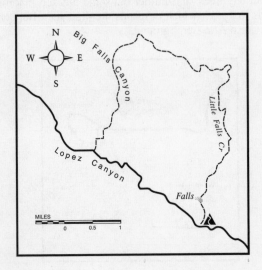

signs to Lopez Lake. Ten miles from the highway, and shortly before entering Lopez Lake Recreation Area, bear right onto Hi Mountain Road. Drive ⅖-mile to Upper Lopez Canyon Road and turn left. You'll drive north, then west, finally bearing right after 6⅕ miles where a sign directs you toward Lopez Canyon. Soon after the pavement ends, you reach the trailhead for Little Falls.

The walk: The creekside trail passes some intriguing pools before reaching a junction in a short ½-mile. The left fork extends 100 feet to the base of Little Falls, while the main path heads right, switchbacking to the top of the falls.

Leaving the falls behind, the path ascends the spring wildflower–strewn wall of the canyon, past purple buckwheat and lots of lupine, soon dropping back down to the creek.

The hike's second mile is a fairly mellow ascent combined with a couple of creek crossings. The last mile is more rigorous as the path emerges from oak woodland onto shadeless slopes and travels to a junction with Hi Mountain Road.

▲ Big Falls

Big Falls Trail

Terrain: Wet, wooded, west-flowing tributary canyon of
Lopez Canyon.

Highlights: Inviting pools, two waterfalls, views from top of
canyon.

Distance: To lower pools and falls is 1 mile round-trip; to
upper falls is 3 miles round-trip with 400-foot elevation
gain; to Hi Mountain Road is 6 miles round-trip with 1,500-
foot elevation gain.

Degree of difficulty: Easy to moderate.

Precautions: Access road impassable in rainy season; abundant poison oak.

Few trails traverse the rugged Santa Lucia Wilderness, an isolated,
little-traveled part of the southern Santa Lucia Mountains. Perhaps
the most enjoyable of pathways is Big Falls, which delivers the destination promised by its name along with a couple of fine swimming holes and a lush, shaded canyon.

Big Falls, paired with its smaller cascading cousin, Little Falls,
adds up to wet and wild adventure.

Getting to the falls can be an adventure in itself. The road up
Lopez Canyon crosses the creek more than a dozen times before
dead-ending at the Big Falls trailhead. A high-clearance vehicle is
required to negotiate the creek crossings, where water often reaches
the bottom of car doors. At times, as you drive to the trailhead, you
might imagine you're a spawning salmon struggling upstream (one
200-yard stretch of road is the same route taken by the creek).

Although freshwater is on every Big Falls hiker's mind, it's saltwater that was the dominant influence in the area several million
years ago. Fossilized scallops and sand dollars embedded in the
nearby hillsides provide evidence of an ancient seashore.

The trail wanders from one bank to another up Big Falls Canyon
Creek, reaching two waterfalls and then ascending the wooded can-
yon to Hi Mountain Road for views of the wilderness and nearby
Lake Margarita.

Hikers looking for a longer excursion can follow a 12-mile loop on Big Falls Trail, Hi Mountain Road, Little Falls Trail, and Lopez Canyon Road.

Directions to trailhead: From Highway 101 in Arroyo Grande, take the Lopez Lake exit and head east on Highway 227, following signs to Lopez Lake. Ten miles from the highway, and shortly before entering Lopez Lake Recreation Area, bear right onto Hi Mountain Road. Drive ⅕-mile to Upper Lopez Canyon Road and turn left. You'll drive north, then west, finally bearing right after 6⅕ miles where a sign directs you toward Lopez Canyon. The pavement ends just before you reach the trailhead for Little Falls. Continue 2 more miles, crossing shallow Lopez Canyon Creek many times before reaching road's end and a small parking area.

The walk: Follow the trail downcreek very briefly and cross it. On the other side, head up Big Falls Canyon in the heavy shade of bay, oak, and sycamore.

Paradisiacal as the canyon seems in places—with maidenhair ferns flourishing above handsome rock pools—profligate poison oak lines the path, which crosses the creek several times. A ½-mile's travel brings you to the lower waterfall, a 50-foot cascade with a pool at its base.

The path continues past the falls on a switchbacking ascent, penetrating a narrow canyon perfumed by bay trees. A mile from the lower falls are the 90-foot-high upper falls, which also drop into a large pool.

Beyond the falls the trail begins a switchbacking ascent, soon reaching a more open area that boasts several shallow pools. Sometimes by midsummer the upper reaches of the creek are dry. A last mile of switchbacking and a serious ascent (1,000-foot gain) brings you to Hi Mountain Road.

Lopez Lake

Blackberry Spring, Turkey Flat Trails

Terrain: Rolling foothills of Santa Lucia Mountains.
Highlights: Fern-lined canyons, superb wildlife-watching.
Distance: Blackberry Spring–Turkey Flat Loop is 1⅓ miles round-trip.
Degree of difficulty: Easy to moderate.
Precautions: Poison oak is plentiful along the trails.

Tucked away in the rolling foothills of the Santa Lucia Mountains, little Lake Lopez offers the hiker some inspiring trails as well as superb bird-watching opportunities.

The lake's purpose is to provide water for the "Five Cities" of the Central Coast. (California trivia buffs, can you name them?) Unlike other reservoir parks, however, Lopez doesn't have that dammed, cement-lined look, and nature-oriented visitors who arrive without a speedboat or jet ski in tow are not regarded by rangers as some lesser life form. On the contrary, Lopez Lake Recreation Area's excellent trail system and educational nature pamphlets could serve as a model for other lake-centered parks.

The best family walk is ¾-mile-long Blackberry Spring Trail. This nature path, keyed to an interpretive pamphlet, provides an introduction to the local flora and suggests how the native Chumash used the area's abundant plant life for food and medicine.

I had a funny moment on this nature trail. No sooner had I paused at interpretive stop 4 and read, "Mule deer are common in the park and frequently seen along the ridge," than a large doe bounded past me.

For a scenic return route, hikers should continue past the last interpretive stop on the nature trail, ascending briefly but steeply to a ridge top and joining signed Turkey Flat Trail. Hundreds of often-raucous wild turkeys roam the park, and this ridge is one of their favorite habitats. Turkey Flat Trail offers a nice view of the lake before descending to the parking area near the entrance station.

Directions to trailhead: From Highway 101 in Arroyo Grande, take the Grand Avenue / Highway 227 exit. Turn right (inland) on Grand (which soon becomes known as East Branch Street) and drive a mile through old-town Arroyo Grande to a signed junction. Highway 227 branches left, but you veer right onto Huasana Road. At a junction in another ½-mile, Huasana Road splits off to the right, but you continue straight onto Lopez Drive and proceed 8 miles to Lopez Lake Recreation Area. Park in the lot behind the entrance station. The day-use fee is four dollars per vehicle.

You'll spot the trailhead for Turkey Ridge Trail on the east side of the parking lot. To reach Blackberry Nature Trail, walk over a footbridge from the parking area to Squirrel Campground and continue 75 yards up the campground road to the signed trailhead on the left.

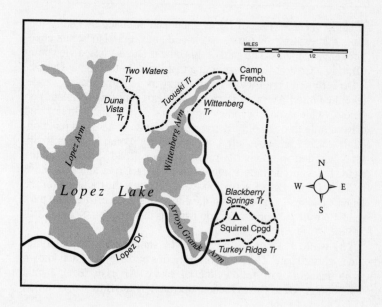

▲ Lopez Lake

Duna Vista Trail

> **Terrain:** Oak woodland, grassland, lakeshore.
> **Highlights:** Central Coast vistas.
> **Distance:** To Duna Vista is 7 miles round-trip with 500-foot elevation gain.
> **Degree of difficulty:** Moderate.

A comprehensive tour of Lopez Lake can be made by taking four trails that explore the park's oak woodlands, grasslands, and chaparral environments. The goal of this hike is Duna Vista, a viewpoint offering a Central Coast panorama that includes the Pismo Dunes.

Directions to trailhead: From Highway 101 in Arroyo Grande, take the Grand Avenue / Highway 227 exit. Turn right (inland) on Grand (which soon becomes known as East Branch Street) and drive a mile through old-town Arroyo Grande to a signed junction. Highway 227 branches left, but you veer right onto Huasana Road. At a junction in another ½-mile, Huasana Road splits off to the right, but you continue straight onto Lopez Drive and proceed 8 miles to Lopez Lake Recreation Area. To reach the trailhead for the Duna Vista trek, continue past the entrance station up the main park road 1½ miles to some roadside parking just before a NO PARKING BEYOND THIS POINT sign.

The walk: Hike up the paved road a short distance to a (sometimes-closed) gate. The road, dirt from this point forward and known as Wittenberg Trail, follows the lakeshore. An easy, level, 1-mile walk brings you to Camp French, operated by the Boy Scouts of San Luis Obispo County.

You'll walk along a fence topped by wooden signs naming the twelve points of Scout law, "Trustworthy, loyal, helpful . . . ," then veer left onto signed Tuouski Trail. After passing the Scouts' campfire circle with the motto BE PREPARED etched into the huge stone hearth, the trail parallels, then follows the "Walk of Eagles" dedicated to Eagle Scouts, including astronaut Ellison Onizuka, who became an Eagle Scout in 1964 and perished in the 1986 space shuttle *Challenger* disaster.

At the edge of Camp French, join signed Tuouski Trail, which follows lakeside bluffs on the north side of the Wittenberg arm of

146

Lopez Lake. (When the lake level is high from winter rains, short stretches of the trail are boggy.) A 1¼ mile of walking from Camp French brings you to the signed junction with Two Waters Trail. A flat, sunny spot here suggests a picnic or rest stop.

Two Waters Trail ascends in earnest ¾-mile up the oak-dotted ridge dividing the Lopez and Wittenberg arms of the lake. At a saddle, signed Duna Vista Trail heads south, climbing another ½-mile to the Duna Vista viewpoint.

After relaxing on the benches and taking in a view stretching from Pismo Beach to the crests of the Santa Lucia Mountains, return the way you came.

One hundred miles of coastline beckon the hiker to explore San Luis Obispo County.

7. San Luis Obispo County Coastline

Along San Luis Obispo's 100 miles of coastline the walking is varied: across wide sandy beaches, around protected bays, over high dunes, and around rugged headlands. Hikers may see bird-watchers gazing at the shimmering tops of eucalyptus trees where great blue herons build their nests, rock hounds gathering moonstones, or clammers digging for Pismo and razor clams.

The southern part of the county's coastline is dominated by windswept sand dunes, the great heaps held in place by ice plant, verbena, grasses, and silver lupine. Because the longshore currents that normally carry sand along the coast are interrupted by rocky headlands, the sand stays in the local area, later to be deposited by the wind on the dunes above the beach.

At Montana de Oro State Park, one of the gems of California's park system, fields of mustard and poppies give the park its "Mountain of Gold" name. Inland areas of the park include Valencia Peak, which offers great Central Coast panoramas, and Coon Creek Canyon, where a stand of the rare Bishop pine thrives.

Morro Bay and its adjacent mudflats are an amazingly fertile wetland, one of the largest and most significant wildlife habitats on the California coast. The bay ranks within the top-ten areas in the nation in terms of numbers of bird species sighted in a single day. Guarding the bay is the much photographed Morro Rock, "The Gibraltar of the Pacific," which stands halfway between Los Angeles and San Francisco.

North of Morro Bay tall bluffs rise above the beach. Land and sea blend into one astounding plateau. Cliff trails follow the edges of grassy coastal terraces, past Cambria Pines, San Simeon, Piedras Blancas, to just south of the Monterey County line. Unlike the theatrical cliffs of Big Sur, these bluffs are accessible; they ebb and flow toward the Coast Highway like the tide, sometimes 20 feet away, sometimes a mile, and always an adventure for those hiking along Land's End.

William Randolph Hearst Memorial State Beach

San Simeon Bay Trail

Terrain: San Simeon Bay.
Highlights: Coastline and castle views.
Distance: 2 miles round-trip.
Degree of difficulty: Easy.

A walk along San Simeon Bay is a nice diversion before or after a tour of La Cuesta Encantada ("The Enchanted Hill"), the famous castle built by newspaper publisher William Randolph Hearst.

In the mid-1860s a severe drought wrecked the Central Coast cattle business and forced many debt-ridden Spanish rancheros to sell their land. Senator George Hearst bought out the rancheros and began developing his family estate.

After the death of William Randolph Hearst in 1951, his heirs donated the beach south of Sebastian General Store for a park. It's a tranquil place; San Simeon Bay provides fairly good refuge from northwest and west winds. The store was established in 1873 and is still in operation.

Directions to trailhead: William Randolph Hearst Memorial State Beach is located on San Simeon Road west of Highway 1. (Hearst Castle is also located on San Simeon Road—east of the highway.) Park in the state beach day-use lot or along San Simeon Road south of Sebastian General Store. Respect private property signs and park only in designated areas.

The walk: Proceed through the picnic ground located in the eucalyptus grove just north of the fishing pier. When you reach the beach, turn upcoast. When the beach begins to arc westward, ascend to a narrow dirt road leading to the top of the wooded bluffs. The road, which narrows to a trail, offers fine coastline and castle views as it curves toward San Simeon Point. From the point are additional breathtaking views to the south of the undeveloped San Luis Obispo County coast.

The path continues around the point on overgrown bluff-top trails, then passes under the boughs of Monterey cypress on a dark tunnel-like trail for ¼-mile before reemerging on the bluffs. The bluff trails grow more and more faint and erratic and you descend a low sand dune to the beach. You can follow the beach until tides and rocks prevent further progress and you meet the Coast Highway quite some distance north.

Hearst Castle
Walking Tours 1, 2, 3, and 4

Hearst Castle (Hearst San Simeon State Historical Monument) offers four fabulous walking tours of the palatial estate of the late newspaper tycoon William Randolph Hearst. More than one million visitors arrive annually to see the collection of world treasures on display in the 130-room castle.

Tour number 1, recommended for first-time visitors, includes the major rooms of the mansion, swimming pools, and gardens. Other tours, restricted to much smaller groups (12 to 15 people), cover the upper levels of the castle, the guest wing, and—my favorite—the gardens, pools, wine cellar, and guest house.

After your walking tour, enjoy a picnic at William R. Hearst Memorial State Beach, located on San Simeon Road west of Highway 1. Nearby Sebastian General Store, established in 1873, sells food and snacks. For recorded tour information call (805) 927–2000. For tour reservations call MISTIX at (800) 444–4445.

California's most popular guided walk explores the many rooms and extensive grounds of Hearst Castle.

San Simeon State Park

San Simeon Creek Trail

Terrain: Wetland, Monterey pine grove, grassy hills.
Highlights: Diverse backcountry of state park.
Distance: 3½ miles round-trip.
Degree of difficulty: Easy to moderate.

What's there to see in San Simeon besides the castle? Thousands of travelers on their way to Hearst Castle ask this question.

The answer is found at San Simeon State Park, which boasts a diversity of scenery from shoreline to Monterey pine forest. Among its amenities are a new trail with interpretive displays, a boardwalk that crosses a wetland, and numerous benches offering a place to rest and observe the tranquil surroundings. The pathway circles the park's San Simeon Creek and Washburn campgrounds. A ¼-mile of the path is wheelchair accessible.

Back in the 1880s, the park's 500 acres of backcountry were part of Ira Whittaker's ranch and dairy operation. Eucalyptus was planted, both as a windbreak and for firewood to fuel the dairy's boiler for cheese making.

The park's botanical highlight is a stand of Monterey pine, part of the famed Cambria Pines, and one of only four native groves left on earth. In winter, Monarch butterflies, more often seen on the Central Coast in eucalyptus trees and other non-native flora, cluster in the park's Monterey pines.

San Simeon Creek is habitat for the endangered red-legged frog and Western pond turtle. Many migratory birds can be counted at the park's seasonal wetland: cinnamon teal, mallards, egrets, and herons.

Directions to trailhead: From Highway 1, just south of the turnoff for San Simeon Creek Campground, turn inland and park at Washburn Day Use Area. Walk inland along the service road to the signed trailhead on your right. Campers can walk to the trailhead—just west of San Simeon Creek bridge—along the campground road.

The walk: The path tours the eastern fringe of the seasonal wetland and soon reaches a boardwalk that leads across it from one viewing area to another. Beyond the boardwalk the trail junctions. The right fork leads southwest ⅕-mile to the Moonstone Gardens

153

restaurant and Highway 1. Along this side trail, eagle-eyed hikers might get a glimpse of Hearst Castle 5 miles to the north.

The main trail climbs onto a flat-topped, Monterey pine–dotted ridge. A sometimes overgrown path detours left (north) 200 yards to a scenic overlook.

Our route descends from the pines into a lush riparian area and turns north. A boardwalk crosses a boggy lowland filled with willow, cottonwood, and a thick understory of wax myrtle and blackberry bushes.

The path next ascends grassy slopes along the eastern boundary of the park. From the former grazing land, you look out over a scene from the California of a century ago: a windmill, pastoral slopes dotted with cows, the unspoiled beauty of the southern Santa Lucia Mountains.

The trail skirts the edge of the campground, then leads west and ascends to an overlook. Savor the mountain vistas, then head southwest on the bluffs above San Simeon Creek.

About ¼-mile from its end, the trail splits. The path you've been following continues above San Simeon Creek back to the day-use area. A second branch crosses the campground road and leads toward the wetland boardwalk, where you turn right and retrace the first five minutes of your walk back to the trailhead.

Moonstone Beach

Moonstone Beach Trail

Terrain: Unique beach of colored rocks.
Highlights: Moonstones; sea otter– and whale-watching.
Distance: From Santa Rosa Creek to Leffingwell Landing
   is 2½ miles round-trip.
Degree of difficulty: Easy.

Named for its moonstones (milky translucent agates), gravelly shored Moonstone Beach is a great place for rock hounds. Moonstones and jaspers—types of quartz—were carried here by streams from the nearby coastal range and then polished by surf and sand.

From the bluffs above Moonstone Beach—part of San Simeon State Beach—the walker may observe sea otters; the beach marks the southern boundary of the California Sea Otter Game Refuge. During January and February, gray whale–watching is excellent here because the giants swim close to shore.

This walk begins at the mouth of Santa Rosa Creek, where there's a small freshwater lagoon. The path winds atop the bluffs above Moonstone Beach and visits Leffingwell Landing, the site of a pier that figured prominently in the nineteenth-century coastal trade and is now a fine picnic area.

Directions to trailhead: From Highway 1, just north of Cambria, turn west on Moonstone Beach Drive. Park at the Santa Rosa Creek day-use area. (Moonstone Beach Drive intersects Coast Highway both north and south of Moonstone Beach.)

The walk: Follow the bluff trail north from the parking area. The rugged headlands are undeveloped, in contrast to "Motel Row" on the east side of Moonstone Beach Drive.

A mile of walking along this beach of colored rocks brings you to the old highway bridge that spans Leffingwell Creek. Just above the creek is a state park day-use area at Leffingwell Landing, where picnic tables are nestled in a sheltered cypress grove. In the 1870s and 1880s, ships unloaded lumber and other goods here for the pioneer settlers who lived near San Simeon Creek.

The path picks up again at the bluff edge past the picnic area and winds through Monterey pine and cypress. Soon you'll be treated to views of Piedras Blancas Lighthouse to the north and Hearst Castle inland. Native American mortar holes are ground into the sandstone bluffs.

You can either descend the bluffs to the beach or angle over to a vista area located close to the point where Moonstone Beach Drive intersects Coast Highway.

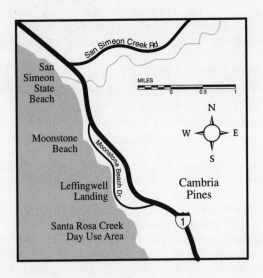

Morro Bay State Park

Black Mountain Trail

> **Terrain:** One of the area's morros (volcanic peaks).
> **Highlights:** Excellent vistas of Morro Bay.
> **Distance:** 3 miles round-trip with 600-foot elevation gain.
> **Degree of difficulty:** Easy.

A series of nine peaks between San Luis Obispo and Morro Bay originated as volcanoes beneath the sea that covered this area some 15 million years ago. After the sea and volcanic explosions subsided, erosion began dissolving the softer mountain material around the volcanic rock, leaving nine volcanic peaks standing high above the surrounding landscape. These volcanic plugs include Islay Peak in Montana de Oro State Park, Hollister Peak, and famed Morro Rock.

Black Mountain, the last peak in the volcanic series before Morro Rock, has a trail that tours a little of everything—chaparral, eucalyptus, oaks, pines, and coastal shrubs. From the mountain's 640-foot summit, you can view the Morro Bay estuary and sand spit and the hills of nearby Montana de Oro State Park.

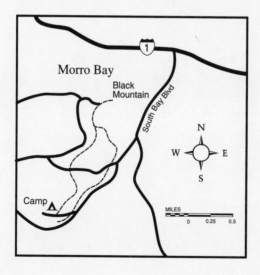

Directions to trailhead: Follow Coast Highway (Highway 1) 12 miles north of San Luis Obispo to the Los Osos / Baywood Park exit just before Morro Bay. Turn south on South Bay Boulevard and go ¾-mile to Morro Bay State Park entrance. Bear left on the first fork beyond the entrance, heading ¾-mile to the campground entrance. Park along the first crossroads inside the campground. Walk up the campground road to the picnic area, where you'll see a pipe gate that indicates the beginning of the trail.

The walk: Follow the Exercise Trail, cross a paved road, and begin ascending the mountain. A mile from the trailhead, there's a junction. Bear left. The route becomes steeper, passing first through coastal shrubs, then conifers. The trail passes a water tank, then switchbacks to the summit.

After enjoying the fine view, you may return the same way or pick up the east fork of the Exercise Trail by backtracking ½-mile to the trail junction, then heading straight (east). You'll discover a eucalyptus grove, where Monarch butterflies cluster. Cross a golf course road and rejoin the eastern section of the Exercise Trail, which returns you to the trailhead.

⚤ Chorro Hill

Chorro Hill Trail

> **Terrain:** Coastal scrub–clad hills.
> **Highlights:** Vistas of Morro Bay wetlands.
> **Distance:** 1¼ miles round-trip.
> **Degree of difficulty:** Easy.

Vistas of the bay lands and Morro Rock are a highlight of this walk to and up Chorro Hill. The 209-foot-high hill is much easier to ascend than neighboring Cabrillo Peak.

As you walk, you get a bird's-eye view of Chorro Creek Estuary, the sprawling wetland created by Toro and Chorro creeks draining in much-meandering fashion to Morro Bay.

Directions to trailhead: From Highway 101 in San Luis Obispo, take the Morro Bay / Highway 1 exit and travel 12 miles north to the outskirts of Morro Bay. Take the signed Morro Bay State Park/ Montana de Oro State Park exit and follow South Bay Boulevard. In ¾-mile the road forks; the right branch leads to the main part of Morro Bay State Park. You'll fork left and continue on South Bay Boulevard another ½-mile to the Cabrillo Peak dirt parking lot on the left (east) side of the road.

The walk: From the parking area, join Quarry Trail for 50 yards, veering left on an unsigned trail, which contours over scrubby slopes above South Bay Boulevard and high above the patterns of water, eelgrass, and mud that make up Chorro Creek Estuary.

After ½-mile the path reaches a dirt road. Turn right and walk up the road. In ¼-mile, another dirt road splits off to the left to the abandoned site of Chorro Willows Group Camp. A trail once led from the camp to Chorro Hill but it has become badly overgrown.

When the road reaches the park boundary fence, angle left and follow a thin trail to the Monterey pine–topped summit of Chorro Hill.

Cabrillo Peak

Quarry, Live Oak, Park Ridge Trails

Terrain: Volcanic "plugs," native grasslands, coastal scrub.
Highlights: Grand Morro Bay and Los Osos Valley views.
Distance: 2 to 4 miles round-trip; 900-foot elevation gain to top of Cabrillo Peak.
Degree of difficulty: Easy hiking around peak; short but strenuous off-trail climb to top of peak.
Precautions: Wear long pants in brushy areas off trail; watch for ticks.

Morro Rock, the much-photographed Central Coast icon, official State Landmark Number 801, and the "Gibraltar of the Pacific," isn't the only morro in town.

Eight more morros—small volcanic peaks—are linked with the famed rock in a chain that stretches from San Luis Obispo to Morro Bay. A couple of these morros (all of which are taller than the photogenic but relatively puny Morro Rock) offer great short hikes.

Geologists say the nine morros originated as volcanoes beneath the sea that covered the area a million years ago. After the sea and volcanic explosions subsided, erosion began dissolving the softer parts of the mountain around the volcanic rock, leaving the nine volcanic peaks standing above the surrounding landscape.

Among the more prominent morros visible to the traveler are Islay Peak east of the San Luis Obispo County Airport and San Luis Mountain towering above the Madonna Inn. The two of most interest to hikers are Cabrillo Peak and Black Mountain, both in Morro Bay State Park.

Cabrillo Peak is a recent addition to the state park. The top of the 911-foot morro affords a terrific 360-degree panorama that includes Morro Rock to the west, the Irish Hills and Los Osos Valley to the south, the chain of Morros going east, and the Santa Lucia Mountains and southern Big Sur backcountry to the north.

The adventurous will bushwhack up trailless Cabrillo Peak. A few faint, zigzag paths—made by use, not design—help the intrepid climber, but it's a make-you-own-way kind of hike to the top. Allow yourself plenty of time to ascend Cabrillo.

At the base of the peak are rolling grasslands with 2 miles or so of trail. Quarry Trail was so named for the rock quarried here and crushed for local roads. Park Ridge Trail explores a group of minor peaks. Striking Park Ridge Rock is a state-park-ranger training site for cliff rescues.

Live Oak Trail meanders among the predominant oak along the San Luis Obispo County coast.

Be sure to check out the morro exhibit at the excellent Morro Bay museum, which also boasts some terrific natural history displays and offers a grand view of Morro Bay.

Directions to trailhead: From Highway 101 in San Luis Obispo, take the Morro Bay / Highway 1 exit and travel 12 miles north to the outskirts of Morro Bay. Take the signed Morro Bay State Park/ Montana de Oro State Park exit and follow South Bay Boulevard. In ¾-mile the road forks; the right branch leads to the main part of Morro Bay State Park. You'll fork left and continue on South Bay Boulevard another ½-mile to the Cabrillo Peak dirt parking lot on the left (east) side of the road.

Morro Bay Sand Spit

Sand Spit Trail

> **Terrain:** Sand dunes, bay shoreline.
> **Highlights:** Views of Morro Rock, Morro Bay.
> **Distance:** 4 miles one way.
> **Degree of difficulty:** Easy to moderate.

Dominating the seascape of Morro Bay is the "Gibraltar of the Pacific," 576-foot-high Morro Rock, first sighted by Juan Cabrillo in 1542. The 50-million-year-old volcanic peak was used as a rock quarry as late as 1969 but is now a wildlife preserve and part of the state park system.

On the inland side of Morro Bay is the state park, which includes a golf course, marina, and superb nature museum.

Morro Bay is made possible by a long, narrow sand spit—one of Central California's special environments. Walkers stride the sand dunes and ridges that separate Morro Bay on the inland side and Estero Bay on the ocean side. Atop some of the higher dunes (about 80 feet above sea level), you'll be treated to good vistas of the bay, Morro Rock, and nearby mountains.

Heather, salt grass, and coyote bush are among the hardy plants surviving in the harsh, wind-lashed environment of the 3-mile-long sand spit. Silver lupine, sea rocket, and evening primrose add seasonal color.

Bird-watchers may spot the snowy plover, which lays its eggs in the sand. On the muddy flats of the spit's bay side, willets, curlews, and sandpipers feed.

Scientists say that a very high percentage of all sea life along the Central Coast originates in Morro Bay Estuary. The triangular-shaped marsh, lined with eelgrass and pickleweed, is an important spawning and nursery habitat for such fish as the California halibut and sand perch. Beneath the surface of the bay are oysters, clams, worms, snails, crabs, and shrimp.

To learn more about the bay's ecology and its animal and plant life, visit the museum in Morro Bay State Park. Exhibits are well done and the panoramic view of the bay is superb.

A key element of this walk can be the Bay Taxi, a water-taxi service between the town of Morro Bay and the north end of the sand spit. The taxi operates May through September, Thursday through Monday, out of Virg's Landing; call (805) 772–1222.

Directions to trailhead: Assuming the Bay Taxi is running, this walk begins in the town of Morro Bay at 1215 Embarcadero.

If you want to arrange a car shuttle or begin your hike at the south end of the sand spit, here's how to reach the south trailhead: from Highway 101 in San Luis Obispo, exit on Los Osos Valley Road and head west through the town of Los Osos. One block after the road curves left to become Pecho Valley Road, turn right on Monarch Lane. Drive to the end of this road and park.

The walk: From the end of the sand spit, where the Bay Taxi lands, walk south along the bay. The shoreline is silty, salty, and quite a contrast to the sandy dunes you'll be crossing farther south.

A mile of bay-side walking brings you to Houseboat Cove. Across the bay from the cove is the Morro Bay museum. Continue another few hundred yards past the cove, then climb over the dunes to the ocean side of the sand spit. Walk south along surf's edge, which is littered with clamshells and sand dollars. After about 2½ miles of travel, as the dunes on your left begin to recede, walk up a valley toward the top of the dunes.

You'll see a large shell mound in the center of the valley, a massive artifact left by the Chumash Indians. They piled clams, cockles, snails, and even land game refuse in these kitchen middens.

For more than three hundred years, Morro Rock has greeted explorers by land and by sea.

163

(Inspect this and other shell mounds on the spit with care; they are protected archaeological sites.) The bountiful marsh is so full of bird, land, and aquatic life that it's easy to imagine a large population of Chumash here; the men hunting rabbits in the dunes, the beautiful baskets of the women overflowing with shellfish.

From the top of the dunes, you'll get a good view of Morro Bay and spit's end at Shark Inlet. Across the bay are the Morros, a series of extinct volcanoes that includes the famous Morro Rock. Rising behind the Morros are the Santa Lucia Mountains, which stretch to Big Sur and beyond. This viewpoint is a good place to turn around and return to the trailhead at the north end of the spit.

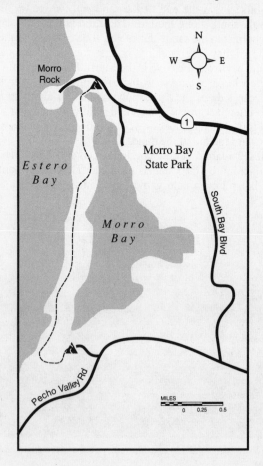

Los Osos Oaks State Reserve

Oak Trail

Terrain: Classic California oak woodland.
Highlights: Magnificent ancient oaks.
Distance: 1 to 2 miles round-trip.
Degree of difficulty: Easy.
Precaution: Poison oak.

Ancient California live oaks, estimated to be 600 to 800 years old, are the highlight of this state reserve in Los Osos Valley near San Luis Obispo. Two miles of trail meander through the old oaks, which have, during their long lifespan, contorted into some unusual shapes.

Botanists say the oak woodland is a culmination of thousands of years of plant succession that has transformed the area from sparsely vegetated sand dunes into a landscape of California live oaks. Though many of the oaks are quite large, some of those growing on the crest of the dunes are dwarfed.

Chumash Indians gathered acorns from the grove. Shell fragments and bits of charcoal are evidence of their frequent encampments.

Meandering along the eastern boundary of the reserve is Los Osos Creek, lined with bay laurel, sycamore, and even some cottonwood trees.

The oaks are full of bird life. Several species perch in the crowns of the trees; others hunt bugs and grubs in the piles of leaves beneath the trees. The chaparral that makes up one-fourth of the reserve is home to quail and many more birds.

Those piles of sticks you see, some several feet high, are woodrat nests. Judging by all those nests, the rarely seen rodent may be the most common animal in the reserve.

Docent-led walks are sometimes scheduled on weekends. While walking in the reserve, stay on the trail; poison oak is abundant.

Directions to trailhead: From Highway 101 on the southern outskirts of San Luis Obispo, exit on Los Osos Valley Road and travel 8 miles to Los Osos Oaks State Reserve on the left side of the road.

The walk: The path crosses a bridge over a trickling creek, passes a plaque thanking, among others, the California State Parks

Foundation for preserving this place, then begins a clockwise loop through the reserve.

The main path winds through the old oaks, wanders near Los Osos Creek, then leads to an overlook of a still-pastoral part of Los Osos Valley. At a couple of trail junctions, you have the opportunity to shorten or extend your walk.

Even tiny tykes enjoy the ancient oaks.

El Chorro County Regional Park

Eagle Peak Trail

Terrain: Grassy hillsides at base of Santa Lucia Mountains.
Highlights: Former dairy farm, now serene pastoral scene.
Distance: 3 miles with 300-foot elevation gain.
Degree of difficulty: Easy to moderate.

A former dairy pasture and U.S. Army training ground now make up El Chorro County Regional Park, located 7 miles north of San Luis Obispo.

Dairy cows grazed these rolling foothills for many years before the federal government obtained the land and established the National Guard's Camp San Luis Obispo. The Army used the canyon and grounds to train troops during World War II and the Korean War. El Chorro became a park in 1972.

About one-third of the 740-acre park is given over to recreational facilities: horseshoe pits, softball fields, picnic areas, and playgrounds. El Chorro's wilder side is explored by a couple of old farm roads and footpaths that meander alongside oak- and sycamore-shaded Dairy Creek and traverse grassy slopes.

The park's most prominent slope is Eagle Peak, which boasts an eagle painted midway up the hill. The eagle was the work of Italian prisoners of war who were confined at Camp San Luis during World War II. The best view of the eagle is from Highway 1. A newly interpreted trail climbs the peak and returns through an oak woodland.

For a longer tour (3 miles) of the park, you can follow Dairy Road, then loop back on trails through the park's grassy slopes and lowlands.

Directions to trailhead: From Highway 101 in San Luis Obispo, take the Highway 1 exit and drive north 7 miles to El Chorro County Regional Park, located just opposite Cuesta College. Park in the Dairy Creek Walk-in Area.

The walk: Head up the paved road (closed to vehicles), which follows Dairy Creek. In ¹/₁₀-mile you'll spot a trail branching right— Eagle Peak Trail. Climb through oak woodland, up a grassy knoll to a hikers' stile. You'll angle toward the peak, contouring around to the west side of the mountain. You'll get a glimpse of the Cal Poly

San Luis Obispo campus—in particular, Design Village, a collection of unusual work by student engineers and architects. From atop Eagle Peak you look out over Highway 1 and the Chorro Valley.

Retrace your steps to a junction with a path descending into an oak woodland. Eagle Peak Trail meanders through the oaks and returns to Dairy Road. Turn left and return to the trailhead.

Cal Poly San Luis Obispo

Poly Canyon Trail

Terrain: Pastoral hills around campus.
Highlights: Botanical garden, architectural and engineering creations, campus vistas.
Distance: 2½ miles round-trip with 300-foot elevation gain.
Degree of difficulty: Easy to moderate.

Founded in 1901, California Polytechnic State University at San Luis Obispo is now in many ways a thoroughly contemporary campus. But the hills surrounding the school still retain their turn-of-the-century pastoral look.

Although the university has long since outgrown its "Cow Poly" nickname, the school still has a large agricultural department and numerous ag majors among its 15,000 students. Behind the modern campus buildings are ranch houses, barns, livestock pens, and grassy slopes grazed by cows.

Nineteenth-century rancher Bartolo Brizziolari owned these hills, and it was for him that the creek and canyon were named. Brizziolari's name remains on the creek, but the canyon today is more often known as Poly Canyon.

After a pleasant ¾-mile walk through the canyon, you may ascend through a botanical garden to Poly Overlook for a view of the university and San Luis Obispo and/or walk through Design Village, a collection of some of the highly creative works of student architects and engineers.

The hiker looking for a 4- to 6-mile workout is encouraged to explore the several miles of trail that travel the slopes above Poly Canyon. Stay on marked trails; the livestock and agricultural fields are part of the University Farm and function as an open-air laboratory.

Directions to trailhead: From northbound Highway 101 in San Luis Obispo, exit on Grand Avenue and travel ½-mile to the campus. Purchase a daily parking permit (only $1.50—extremely inexpensive by big-city, big-campus standards) at the entry kiosk and ask for the latest parking tips. Continue ³⁄₁₀-mile to North Perimeter Road and turn right. You'll spot Poly Canyon Road (where the walk begins) on your right, but there's no public parking here. During the college summer session, your best bet for parking is nearby Lot R–1, located directly behind the college residence halls. Another option is the metered 90-minute parking next to Plant Operations.

The walk: Take the dirt road on the east bank of Brizziolari Creek. While the creek bed is heavily vegetated, the road is far more exposed and sunny. After a mellow ¼-mile ascent, you can choose between two paths. The path on the left passes under a handsome stone arch into Design Village and loops past two dozen fascinating architectural and engineering projects, including an underground house, a geodesic dome, and a pyramid.

The path on the right crosses a footbridge into a (mostly undeveloped) botanical garden. Take East Canyon Trail to aptly named Yucca Ridge Trail, ascending briefly but steeply to Poly Canyon Overlook on slopes dotted with our Lord's candles. From the overlook, you can trace the course of Poly Canyon, regard the red-tiled roofs of the university, and count the cows grazing in the fields below.

Bishop Peak

Bishop Peak Trail

Terrain: Rocky, oak-dotted volcanic peak.
Highlights: Grand Central Coast vistas.
Distance: 2 miles round-trip.
Degree of difficulty: Short but strenuous.
Precautions: Descending the peak's boulders can be even
   more difficult than climbing them.

Bishop Peak is one of the Morros—that chain of nine volcanic
peaks extending from the city of San Luis Obispo to Morro Bay. At
one time all the morros were privately owned, but over the years
several have been acquired by the state.

In 1980, 150 acres of the upper ramparts of Bishop Peak were donated to the California State Parks Foundation. (The lower part of
the peak, as well the surrounding area, is still privately held, so hikers should be on their best behavior—and give thanks to the owner
who allows access to the peak.)

Bishop Peak was so named by the padres of Mission San Luis
Obispo because the three stony points on the peak resembled the
headpiece of Bishop Saint Louis (San Luis).

From the granite crown of the 1,546-foot peak, hikers get grand
views of the pastoral, Hereford-dotted countryside, along with vistas of the Cal Poly San Luis Obispo campus and the Morro Bay
coastline.

This climb is a popular workout with the local college students.
And indeed it's a climb: the first two-thirds of the trip is on a very
steep trail; the last third is trailless boulder-scrambling.

Bishop Peak, under the stewardship of the San Luis Obispo County
Parks Department, may one day be hiked from Highway 1. Call the
department for more information.

Directions to trailhead: From Highway 101 in San Luis Obispo,
exit on Los Osos Road and head west to Foothill Boulevard. Turn
north (right) and proceed 1½ miles to an unsigned turnout on the
left. The turnout, which has parking for a dozen cars, is at the base
of Bishop Peak. Duck under the barbed-wire fence and join the obvious wide path leading toward the peak.

(A second Bishop Peak trailhead is off Foothill Boulevard about ⅖-mile south of Patricia Drive opposite the Calvary Baptist Church.)

The walk: Follow the wide, mown path through grassy fields. It's a steep ascent up the mustard- and thistle-dotted hillside to an oak grove. Next, climb another 150 yards to a second line of oaks.

Beyond the oak groves, an intermittent trail winds around large granite boulders. Keep climbing (watch for poison oak) and you'll finally gain the top.

Enjoy the grand coastal panorama from the pine-forested headlands of Cambria to the Nipomo Dunes to Point Sal.

Laguna Lake

Laguna Lake Loop Trail

> **Terrain:** Small natural lake, surrounding grassy hills.
> **Highlights:** Bird-watching in mellow park.
> **Distance:** 1½ miles.
> **Degree of difficulty:** Easy.

One of the San Luis Obispo County's few remaining natural lakes, Laguna is a favorite spot for birds—and their watchers. Nesting birds include pied-billed grebes, great blue herons, and snowy egrets. More than 100 bird species have been identified at the lake, including ducks (dabbling and diving), coots, and cormorants.

Laguna Lake (a redundancy since *laguna* is the Spanish word for lake) offers an easy family walk through the park and along the lakeshore. The mostly flat path provides good vistas of the lake and surrounding hills—in particular, 1,292-foot Cerro San Luis Obispo, one of the famed volcanic morros.

One way to explore the park is by following the paved park road northwest by the lakeshore, then joining the dirt exercise trail leading by fenced pastureland. Back toward the park entrance near a line of eucalyptus, a hikers' stile invites you to travel the grassy slopes and rock outcroppings next to the park. You can improvise a loop by beginning with the exercise trail and returning through the pasture.

Directions to trailhead: From Highway 101 in San Luis Obispo, exit on Madonna Road and head southwest ½-mile to the entrance to Laguna Lake Park on the right. Drive to the parking lot next to the restrooms and playground.

Montana de Oro Dunes

Dune Trail

Terrain: Bluffs, dunes, rocky reef.
Highlights: Hazard Canyon tide pools, lonely beach.
Distance: To Hazard Canyon Reef is 2½ miles round-trip; to
  Shark Inlet is 6½ miles round-trip.
Degree of difficulty: Moderate.

Most park visitors head for the well-known bluffs south of Spooners Cove; however, another attraction north of the cove awaits the adventuresome explorer—a magnificent coastline of reefs, ravines, and dunes extending all the way to Morro Bay.

Trails travel the bluffs just north of Spooners Cove, dipping in and out of ravines on a series of horse and surfer trails. Your improvised route provides fine overlooks of handsome (and accessible) pocket beaches and rocky coves. If it's low tide, you might want to hike for stretches along the beach.

Bluff-top trails bring you to narrow Hazard Canyon, where you join a canyon trail, following it through aromatic eucalyptus, blessed in autumn with congregations of monarch butterflies, down to the beach.

The mighty cliffs and dunes here were the site of practice invasions by America's troops-in-training during World War II. In 1995 the shores were again disturbed by explosions, this time by a bomb squad that located—and detonated—the what is hopefully last of the "unexploded ordnance" left behind from these war games of a half-century ago. (The author had walked these shores since Scout days in the 1960s, blissfully unaware of any potentially disturbing ordnance.)

For a shorter ramble you can walk as far as Hazard Canyon. To partake of more of the majesty of this coast, you can follow either bluff or beach to the southernmost tip of Morro Bay.

The walk lends itself to improvisation. Spring wildflower bloom? Enjoy the bluffs. Low tide? Walk the beach.

Directions to trailhead: Look for a small grassy parking area off Pecho Valley Road, just north of Spooners Cove. It's just across the road from the start of the Ridge Trail. Alternative parking, if this small lot is full, is available at a horse-trailer parking area a short distance north on Pecho Valley Road.

The walk: Signed Dune Trail has two branches: a left branch that makes a half-circle above Spooners Cove and a more direct, right branch that heads north. The two join in ¼-mile.

Dune Trail stays behind (on the inland side of) the dunes. Several sandy side trails invite you to climb to the top of the dunes for a look at what's below. After 1¾ miles of sandy trail, you'll reach Hazard Canyon Trail and descend ¼-mile to the beach.

Along the shore of Hazard Canyon Beach you'll find tide pools, flat rocks for picnicking, and superb surfing. Also at the beach are

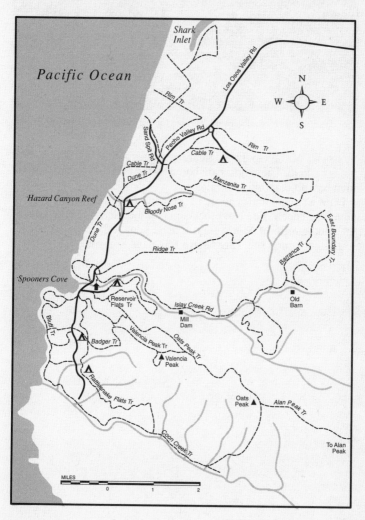

Spooners Cove trails provide plenty of room for improvisational exploration.

thousands of wave-polished sandstone rocks with Swiss cheese–like holes in them. These holes are bored by the piddock, an industrious member of the mollusk family.

Dune Trail continues north, but perhaps a more enjoyable walk is along the beach. You can beachcomb all the way to Sharks Inlet at the southern tip of Morro Bay. Extend your walk even farther by walking the sand spit. (See Morro Bay Sand Spit walk.)

▲

Hazard Canyon

Bloody Nose, Manzanita, Hazard Canyon, Cable Trails

Terrain: Steep slopes of Hazard Canyon.
Highlights: Eucalyptus woodland, Morro Bay vistas.
Distance: 7¾-mile loop with 700-foot elevation gain.
Degree of difficulty: Moderate to strenuous.

The Hazard Canyon walk links several paths and environments in the northern part of Montana de Oro State Park. Trails explore manzanita-blanketed sandy slopes and a eucalyptus woodland. Views from upper Hazard Canyon include Morro Bay and surrounding communities, as well as the distant peaks of Los Padres National Forest.

The land north of Spooners Cove was once owned by dairyman Alexander S. Hazard. Like many a California entrepreneur of his era, he hoped to profit from the rapidly developing state's need for timber. Hazard planted thousands of fast-growing eucalyptus in the canyon that now bears his name. Years later, Hazard and fellow eucalyptus tree farmers found to their dismay that eucalyptus wood was a poor and unsellable building material.

Floods and fires in the 1940s wiped out what had been Hazard's dairy buildings, but his eucalyptus forest remains, offering shade to passing hikers.

Directions to trailhead: From Pecho Valley Road, park in the lot on the west side of the road, opposite the signed entrance to Camp Keep and the park residence area. A path leads from the lot to Hazard Canyon. To begin this hike, cross Pecho Valley Road and walk up the road to Camp Keep.

The walk: Follow the dirt road to Camp Keep, a facility used by Kern County schoolchildren. As you approach the camp, bear left at a dirt road leading through eucalyptus to signed Bloody Nose Trail.

The trail narrows as it turns inland. With the roar of the breakers behind you, the path crosses Hazard Creek, then ascends out of the canyon. From this perspective Hazard Canyon looks very steep indeed. The path soon descends back into the canyon. Look up to your right and notice the bald patches where slides have occurred on the steep canyon walls.

You'll cross Hazard Creek and ascend briefly to a junction, 1 mile from the trailhead. The left fork (your return route) leads northwest toward Cable Trail. Take the signed right fork, Manzanita Trail, and begin a moderate to steep eastbound ascent over sandy and shale slopes clad with manzanita. After 1¾ miles, you'll pass two opportunities to joining East Boundary Trail and instead stay with Manzanita Trail as it makes an almost 180-degree turn and then descends 1¼ mile to an intersection with Hazard Canyon Road.

Turn left and follow the road ¾-mile to the entrance to Horse Camp. Descend the camp road to its end at the last campsite and join Cable Trail as it heads southwest over sandy terrain through eucalyptus forest.

Near Pecho Valley Road, a trail to the beach heads west, but you stay with aptly named Cable Trail (it follows an underground telephone cable) paralleling Pecho Valley Road. The trail dips into a drainage, then climbs a creek bank over a mighty fallen eucalyptus and begins ascending through an impressive eucalyptus forest. A ½-mile climb brings you back to the junction with Manzanita and Bloody Nose trails. Taking the latter path, you retrace your steps a mile back to the trailhead.

Montana de Oro Bluffs

Bluff Trail

Terrain: Dramatic coastal bluffs.
Highlights: Spring wildflowers—a "mountain of gold."
Distance: 4 miles round-trip.
Degree of difficulty: Easy.

Atop the Montana de Oro State Park bluffs grow fields of mustard and poppies that give the park its "Mountain of Gold" name.

At the turn of the century, the greater portion of what is now the state park was part of the Spooner Ranch. The most popular beach in the park is Spooners Cove; its isolation made it an ideal landing spot for *contrabandistas* during the Spanish era, and for bootleggers during Prohibition.

While walking the bluffs, you may see harbor seals venturing ashore or otters diving for food beyond the surf line. Bird-watchers delight in the pelicans, albatross, cormorants, and crimson-billed black oystercatchers.

Inland areas of the park include Valencia Peak, which offers great Central Coast panoramas, and Coon Canyon, where a stand of Bishop pine thrives. The park's campground occupies the bluffs above a small creek; the visitor center is the old Spooner ranch house.

Directions to trailhead: From Highway 101, exit on Los Osos Valley Road, continuing northwest for 12 miles until the road turns south to become Pecho Valley Road, which leads to Montana de Oro State Park. There's parking at Spooners Cove. The trail begins 100 yards south of the turnoff for the campground on the west side of Pecho Valley Road.

The walk: The path crosses a dry creek on a footbridge and leads up to the bluffs overlooking Spooners Cove.

A ½-mile from the trailhead, a short fork to the right leads to Coralina Cove, bedecked with sea-polished broken shells and beautiful beach pebbles. The crystal-clear tide pools are full of anemones, starfish, mussels, and colorful snails.

Continuing on Bluff Trail, you'll cross a wooden bridge. A mile from the trailhead is Quarry Cove, a fine tide-pool site. The wide

179

trail, lined with thistle and New Zealand spinach, eventually brings you to an overlook above some sea caves. Beyond is Grotto Rock.

You may return the same way or cross Pecho Valley Road to the trailhead for Coon Creek Trail.

Islay Creek

Islay Creek, Ridge Trails

Terrain: Grassy heights of San Luis Mountains.
Highlights: Largest and best of Central California's state
parks, spring wildflower blooms, excellent coastal vistas.
Distance: 8½-mile loop with 900-foot elevation gain.
Degree of difficulty: Moderate.
Precautions: Muddy trails, poison oak.

Montana de Oro's 7 miles of coast is so splendid that most first-
time visitors hardly give a thought to the big state park's backcountry. Some long, and usually lonely, trails wind through the mustard-
and buttercup-bedecked mountains of gold.

One of my favorite walks in this part of California is a loop
through the northern part of the park. Sweeping grasslands, stands
of oak, and commanding coastal views of Morro Bay are some of
the highlights of this hike.

Directions to trailhead: From Highway 101 in San Luis Obispo,
exit on Los Osos Valley Road, continuing northwest for 12 miles
until the road turns south to become Pecho Valley Road, which
leads to Montana de Oro State Park. You'll leave your vehicle at a
parking lot on the right (ocean) side of the road, just north of Islay
Creek. The trailhead is 200 feet farther, on the left (inland) side of
the road.

The walk: From the signed trailhead at a steel vehicle gate, walk
up the well-maintained ranch road. A ¼-mile along you'll spot a
handsome outcropping of Monterey shale, formed millions of years
ago beneath the sea.

A mile's hike from the trailhead brings you to a junction with
Reservoir Flats Trail. A ¼-mile farther, you'll see a right-forking
side trail that leads down the banks of Islay Creek to two waterfalls.

At the 2-mile mark, Islay Creek forks and, as the main fork goes
right, our trail goes left along the north fork. Along the road are
huge coffeeberry plants, purple nightshade, and flowering sage.
Three-quarters of a mile past the creek fork is an abandoned barn.

A short way past the barn, the trail forks. To the right, well-named
East Boundary Trail heads east, then swings north along the park's

east boundary. The left fork, Barranca Trail, stays with the creek canyon and heads north. Take either trail; they meet again in ¾-mile.

Five miles from the trailhead, you'll come to another junction. Take the left (west) fork, Ridge Trail. (The right fork, Manzanita Trail, is also a delightful way back to the coast. It brings the hiker to Pecho Valley Road at a point ½-mile north of the trailhead.)

Ridge Trail is indeed a ridge route. It crosses the shoulder of 1,076-foot Hazard Peak (named for pioneer dairyman Alexander S. Hazard, not for any dangers lurking atop the small mountain).

As you descend the ridge back to the trailhead, enjoy the views of Morro Rock, Morro Sand Spit, and on especially clear days, the southern Big Sur Coast.

Oats Peak

Oats Peak Trail

Terrain: Grassland; sandstone outcroppings.
Highlights: Vistas of park and coast.
Distance: From Pecho Valley Road to Oats Peak is 5½ miles
round-trip with 1,300-foot elevation gain; to Alan Peak is
11½ miles round-trip with 1,600-foot elevation gain.
Degree of difficulty: Moderate to strenuous.
Precautions: Plenty of ticks in brushy areas along the trail.

Oats Peak, no doubt named for the fields of wild oats growing on
the slopes of the San Luis Range, offers a good view of the Central
Coast as well as some of the nearby inland valleys and population
centers.

An out-and-back journey to 1,373-foot Oats Peak is a nice workout—or you can opt for two longer trips. One of my favorite options is to take the Oats Peak Connector Trail on a wicked 1¹⁄₁₀-mile
descent to Coon Creek Trail. (See Coon Creek walk.)

From Oats Peak, ambitious hill climbers can continue another 3
miles along a ridgeline to viewful 1,649-foot Alan Peak.

Directions to trailhead: Oats Peak Trail begins at the parking
area located off the campground road just beyond park headquarters.

The walk: For the first ¼-mile, the path is shared with Reservoir
Flats–bound hikers. After a short walk past coastal shrub and sandstone outcroppings, you'll reach a fork. Reservoir Flats Trail veers
left and your Oats Peak Trail heads right. After another ¼-mile of
travel, you'll pass a connector trail on your right leading south to
the Valencia Peak Trail.

A mile from the trailhead is a lush willow-lined area around a
spring. With Valencia Peak on your right in the near distance, you'll
climb an earnest ½-mile, passing a junction with Valencia Peak
Trail. The path becomes more gentle and you'll get over-the-left-
shoulder views of Morro Bay.

A bit more than 2 miles along, the trail dips, then begins its final
½-mile climb to the summit of Oats Peak. Enjoy the views from the
often windy peak.

Just below (eastward) is a trail junction. Oats Peak Trail swings south, plunging steeply to a junction with Coon Creek Trail. (It's a much easier route this way than the trek up to Oats Peak from Coon Creek!)

Three more miles away to the east is Alan Peak. Following the north side of a ridge, Alan Peak Trail delivers you to another terrific vista point.

Reservoir Flats

Reservoir Flats Loop Trail

Terrain: Grassy hills, riparian area along Islay Creek.
Highlights: Family walk, sampler of park attractions.
Distance: 2-mile loop.
Degree of difficulty: Easy.

One of Montana de Oro State Park's fine family walks is the loop around the campground via Reservoir Flats and Islay Creek. Reservoir Flats Loop Trail offers a taste of the park's backcountry—a lush, willow-lined creek and grassy hills and hollows.

Reservoir Flats is really a grassy bowl that forms a shallow pool during the rainy season. Historical evidence suggests that the little lake was more expansive a hundred years ago when the water table was higher.

The land around Islay Creek was purchased in 1892 by Alden B. Spooner, Jr., who began a dairy operation. The family's Pecho Ranch and Stock Company built barns, a ranch house, and a creamery. A waterwheel powered a separator that produced butter and cream.

Directions to trailhead: Signed Reservoir Flats Loop Trail begins from a small parking area just up the campground road from Montana de Oro State Park headquarters.

The walk: The path begins a modest ascent, rising in ³⁄₁₀-mile to a signed junction with Oats Peak Trail (which swings southeast). A short walk farther on, Reservoir Flats Loop Trail brings you to the Flats themselves.

Three-quarters of a mile from the trailhead, the path climbs to a view of the campground and of Spooners Cove. A bit more than a mile out, the trail splits. The right fork drops 100 yards to Islay Creek, then crosses the creek to Islay Road.

Reservoir Flats Loop Trail angles west (left) and follows the south bank of Islay Creek. The trail travels along the creek to the east end of the park campground. Follow the campground road ¼-mile back to the trailhead.

Valencia Peak

Valencia Peak Trail

Terrain: Coastal scrub– and grass-covered marine terraces.
Highlights: Springtime blooms—the "mountain of gold" that gave the park its name.
Distance: From park headquarters to Valencia Peak is 4 miles round-trip with 1,300-foot elevation gain.
Degree of difficulty: Moderate.

From a distance, you might suspect that 1,345-foot Valencia Peak is one of the morros—those distinct cone-shaped mountains that punctuate the San Luis Obispo County coast south of Morro Bay. However, Valencia Peak rose out of the sea in relatively recent geologic time. Geologists believe the processes that fashioned the mountain-tilting, folding, and upheaval occurred only five million years ago.

The peak's oceanic origins are revealed by its upper slopes, which were once beaches. You can find strands of beach sand and rocks that have been bored out by clams. Atop the mountain are fossil shells.

By some accounts, the state park is named for Valencia Peak, which becomes a "mountain of gold" as a result of spring-blooming mustard and California poppies.

This walk switchbacks over what were once sea cliffs to the top of Valencia Peak, named after an Indian family who lived nearby in the years after the mission period. On fog-free days, the view of the Central Coast from Point Sal to Piedras Blancas is inspiring.

Directions to trailhead: Signed Valencia Peak Trail begins from Pecho Valley Road, just south of Montana de Oro State Park headquarters and the campground road.

The walk: The trail follows a grassy area along Pecho Valley Road a short distance, then turns inland and starts upslope to the east. Soon you'll be able to distinguish a series of marine terraces on the mountain. In spring, lupine, mustard, Indian paintbrush, and a host of other wildflowers cover the coastal slope.

Three-quarters of a mile along, you'll pass an old jeep road. The road's left fork leads to Oats Peak Trail; the right fork (Badger Trail) leads back to Pecho Valley Road.

Valencia Peak Trail dips in and out of a dry gully and begins switchbacking over outcroppings of Monterey shale, traces of former sea cliffs. The trail levels out, then begins switchbacking again, more steeply this time. The trail forks a bit below the peak; both trails go to the summit. Here you'll look out over the (mostly) unspoiled coast. You can see the 20-million-year-old volcanic peaks of Morro Rock, Hollister Peak, and Black Mountain.

Look for fossils, enjoy the view, and return the same way.

Coon Creek

Coon Creek Trail

Terrain: Lush coastal canyon.
Highlights: Rare Bishop pine; mellow family walk.
Distance: 5 miles round-trip with 200-foot elevation gain.
Degree of difficulty: Easy to moderate.
Precautions: Often extraordinary amounts of poison oak along this trail.

Coon Creek is a year-round stream that winds through the Irish Hills along a lush canyon to the sea. The vegetation is so thick in the canyon that walkers often pass within a few feet of the creek, hear its murmuring, yet are unable to see it.

Ancient Bishop pines line Coon Creek Canyon, which teems with wildlife—black-tailed deer, rabbits, possum, and, of course, raccoons.

This walk, one of the nicest in Montana de Oro State Park, follows the creek, crossing it a half-dozen times. Occasionally, the trail passes through meadowland seasonally blanketed with fiddleneck, poppies, mustard, and monkey flowers.

Directions to trailhead: Follow Pecho Valley Road (the main park road) to its end at the signed trailhead.

The walk: The path descends a short way into a shallow canyon, then climbs a ridge for a brief shoreline glimpse. The trail soon ventures into Coon Creek Canyon. You can hear but not see the creek on your right. The trail is choked with maple, willow, mugwort, and poison oak. A ½-mile from the trailhead stand some Bishop pines.

Crossing and recrossing the creek, the trail leads among live oaks covered with moss. At the 2-mile mark, you ascend a short distance into an exposed grassland that displays abundant wildflowers in spring.

A few hundred feet from trail's end, on your left, is an intersection with Oats Peak Connector Trail, which ascends a very steep 1¹⁄₁₀ miles (800-foot elevation gain) to a junction with eastbound Alan Peak Trail and westbound Oats Peak Trail.

Coon Creek Trail ends in a mixed stand of old oaks and cedars. Here you'll find the crumbling remains of an old shack.

On old topographic maps, Coon Creek Trail is shown extending several more miles along the creek; alas, impenetrable thickets of poison oak deny passage these days.

Ambitious hikers intent on looping back via Oats Peak can take a very steep 1¹⁄₁₀-mile connector trail. This path gains 1,000 feet in elevation as it climbs through manzanita and other thick brush before intersecting Oats Peak Trail a few hundred feet east of the 1,373-foot summit of Oats Peak.

Point San Luis Lighthouse
Pecho Coast Trail

Terrain: Irish Hills, dramatic coastal bluffs.
Highlights: Guided tour, historic lighthouse. Watchable
  wildlife includes seabirds, seals, and otters.
Distance: 7¼ miles round-trip with 400-foot elevation gain.
Degree of difficulty: Moderate.

Between Montana de Oro State Park and Avila Beach are 10 miles
of California coast that nobody knows, where nobody goes.

The reason for the area's obscurity is that this land has been privately held since Spanish Mission days. For three decades or so,
public access has been strictly forbidden because of a very security-
conscious landowner: Pacific Gas and Electric, whose Diablo Canyon Nuclear Power Plant is in the middle of this pristine stretch of
coast.

Pecho Coast Trail allows limited access to this coast. The pathway climbs the steep bluffs above Avila Beach to the historic Point
San Luis, then crosses a coastal terrace to an oak woodland. The
Nature Conservancy, which provides interpretive services in this
region and whose area office is in San Luis Obispo, leads twice-
weekly hiking tours along the trail. Reservations are required.

Diablo and other coastal canyons were the hunting grounds of the
native Chumash and their predecessors, who inhabited this region
more than 9,000 years ago. In 1968, PG&E began construction of
the controversial Diablo Canyon Nuclear Power Plant. Engineering
difficulties and court challenges, as well as mass demonstrations
over the building of reactors close to an active earthquake fault,
slowed but did not stop the plant, which opened in 1986.

The $300,000 pathway project was funded by PG&E; the trail
was a concession negotiated by the California Coastal Commission
when it granted the utility permission for a 1983 construction pro-
ject. The California Conservation Corps built and engineered Pecho
Coast Trail.

A trail highlight is a tour of the old Point San Luis Obispo Lighthouse, built in 1890. The "Victorian Lady," as it's known to locals,
warned ships off the rocky coast until 1975, when the facility was
deactivated and replaced by an automated beacon.

The Nature Conservancy docents who lead the tours are enthusiastic folks who share lots of nature lore and local history. Those hikers wanting a workout more strenuous than a nature walk are apt to get fidgety during the guided tour, which is geared to the slowest hikers and takes 6 to 7 hours to cover 7 miles.

Directions to trailhead: From Highway 101, a little north of Pismo Beach and a little south of San Luis Obispo, exit on Avila Beach Drive and follow it 4 miles to the gated entrance road of the Diablo Canyon Nuclear Power Plant. Park along Avila Beach Drive and join one of the Nature Conservancy docents who will guide you along the trail.

For a trail brochure and information about free hiking tours, write to The Nature Conservancy, Central Coast Preserves, P.O. Box 15810, San Luis Obispo, CA 93406, or call (805) 541–TREK.

The walk: Don't judge a trail by its trailhead. At first, Pecho Coast Trail appears like the route to a minimum-security prison. Soon, however, it leaves the gates and barbed wire behind and begins ascending the dramatic bluffs above San Luis Obispo Bay via a narrow asphalt road.

Veering from the road, you'll join signed Pecho Coast Trail and get great over-the-shoulder views of the bay's three piers (from north to south: Harford, Unocal, Avila), as well as Avila Beach. Pacific currents carry sand past mostly rocky San Luis Obispo Bay, but deposit sand en masse at Pismo Beach and its southern neighbors, Grover Beach and Oceano. Forming a dramatic backdrop to these beaches are the sparkling Nipomo Dunes.

The path rejoins the asphalt road for a short distance and soon reaches the lighthouse. After learning about the lonely lives of the lighthouse keepers and their families, you'll hit the trail again, traveling north atop the coastal bluffs.

Pecho Coast Trail dips down to the coastal terrace, where you'll pass among grazing cattle. Advancing very quietly, you'll sneak a peek at the harbor seals and sea otters that sometimes haul out onto the shore at low tide.

The path loops through an oak grove, where you'll take a lunch break. After lunch, you'll return the way you came. The panorama of San Luis Obispo Bay is even better on the way back.

Pismo Dunes

Pismo Dunes Trail

Terrain: Wind-sculpted sand dunes.
Highlights: Largest set of coastal dunes in California.
Distance: 2 or more miles round-trip.
Degree of difficulty: Easy to moderate.

Pismo Beach has a little something for everyone. Digging for the famed Pismo clam (now scarce) has long been a popular pastime. Two campgrounds at the state beach are favorites of families looking for weekend getaways. Pismo Dunes State Vehicular Recreation Area is a sandy playground for street vehicles and off-highway vehicles.

For walkers, the attraction is Pismo State Dunes Natural Preserve, a region of tall sand hills where vehicles are prohibited and you can wander for miles in a Sahara-by-the-sea. Often referred to as the Nipomo Dunes these days, they stretch 18 miles from the northern end of Pismo State Beach to Point Sal State Beach.

The dunes, 1 to 3 miles wide, are a dynamic ecosystem: they've been building up, shifting in response to the prevailing northwest winds, for the last 18,000 years or so. Some dunes continue to be formed today. The active, moving ones are those with little or no vegetation.

Flowers, plants, and grasses are vital to the dune ecosystem because they stabilize the drifting sands. Brightening the dunes in the springtime are yellow and magenta sand verbena, coreopsis, daisies, and white-fringed aster.

During the Great Depression of the 1930s, the dunes were home to the Dunites, a motley collection of writers, artists, hermits, nudists, and astrologers who lived in driftwood shacks and published their own magazine called *The Dune Forum.* Shifting sands buried the Dunite community as they had earlier buried more elaborate developments.

This walk explores the dune preserve inland from Pismo Beach State Vehicular Recreation Area. The shoreline itself is often a traffic jam of cars, trucks, and off-highway vehicles filled with families, low-riders, and what seems to be half the population of Bakersfield.

A few hundred yards inland from this shoreline sigalert, it's quiet, even lonely. Virtually no one bothers to walk into the dune preserve to see nature's handiwork.

Directions to trailhead: From Highway 101 in Arroyo Grande, exit on Grand Avenue and follow it westward to Highway 1. Head south a mile to the community of Oceano, just south of Grover Beach, and turn west on Pier Avenue. The Pismo Dunes State Vehicular Recreation Area entrance station is a short distance ahead. If you have a four-wheel-drive or high-clearance vehicle, you can pay a fee here and drive onto the beach. (Pismo boosters claim their beach is the only one in California where the sand is firm enough to support travel by standard automobiles, even low-slung family cars, but I have my doubts; I've seen a lot of cars stuck in the sand.)

If you're driving, head south about ½-mile. The beach is signed with numbered markers. Park near the first marker you see—Marker 1.

If you're not keen on driving the beach, park along Pier Avenue short of the entrance kiosk. You may then (1) walk ½-mile south along water's edge (not as treacherous as it looks from a distance with all those vehicles on the beach) to the dune entrance; or (2) walk ¼-mile or so along Strand Way, a residential street paralleling the beach, then continue south along the banks of Arroyo Grande Creek, which near its mouth also parallels the beach, to the dune preserve entrance.

(If you park on Pier Avenue, add about another mile to your walk.)

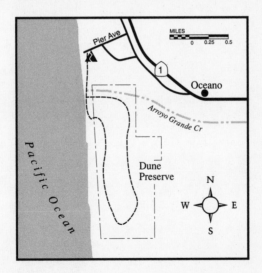

The walk: Head inland to the fence that marks the boundary of the Pismo State Dunes Natural Preserve. Take any of the meandering southbound trails that cross the dunes. A ridgeline of sand shields walkers from the sights and sounds of the busy beach below.

Continue southward along the shrub-dotted base of the dunes for a mile or so, then ascend out of the foredunes toward the crest of the great dunes to the east. You can then return north on the crest of the large dunes.

When you reach Arroyo Grande Creek, the northern boundary of the preserve, return to the beach. At this point, you're about 200 yards north of Marker 1, so head south back to the trailhead.

Oceano Lagoon

Guiton Trail

Terrain: Freshwater lagoon.
Highlights: Interpreted nature trail.
Distance: ½-mile loop.
Degree of difficulty: Easy.

A ½-mile loop trail around Oceano Lagoon offers a good introduction to the special world of a freshwater marshland.

The lagoon was dredged out of once-extensive marshland during the 1920s. The marsh is believed to be the remnant of a freshwater lake fed by runoff from coastal creeks.

Harold Guiton, for whom the trail was named, donated the lagoon to the state park system in 1935 and worked for the formation of Pismo State Beach. The dozen-stop nature trail highlights the diverse lagoon plant life and the ways that the native Chumash, early inhabitants of this area, used the plants for food and medicine.

Directions to trailhead: The trail begins just off Pier Avenue in Pismo State Beach's Oceano Campground. Ask for an interpretive pamphlet at the campground entry station.

Nipomo Dunes

Oso Flaco Beach Trail

Terrain: Sand dunes, tiny lakes.
Highlights: One of California's largest dune fields; great bird-watching at Oso Flaco lakes.
Distance: To beach is 2 miles round-trip; to Santa Maria River mouth is 8 miles round-trip.
Degree of difficulty: Easy to moderate.

The Nipomo Dunes are one of the largest relatively undisturbed dune complexes in California. The dunes, which extend from the northern end of Pismo State Beach to Point Sal just north of Vandenberg Air Force Base, were in 1974 declared a national landmark.

In 1904, Oceano boasted beach cottages, a wharf, and mammoth La Grande Beach Pavilion. The developer's grandiose plans of turning Oceano into a tourist mecca did not materialize and the pavilion, wharf, and cottages were buried beneath advancing dunes.

This walk passes between Oso Flaco and Lower Oso Flaco lakes to the dunes, then travels down to the beach. The trail and lakes area of the dunes are operated by The Nature Conservancy.

Directions to trailhead: From Highway 1, some 9½ miles south of Oceano and 3 miles north of Highway 166, turn west on Oso Flaco Road and follow it 3½ miles to road's end at the dunes. The Nature Conservancy collects a parking fee from a kiosk at the trailhead.

The walk: Follow the narrow, cottonwood-shaded paved road as it passes between the "big" and "little" Oso Flaco lakes. Rails and grebes nest at water's edge, and sandpipers and a rather raucous duck population winter here.

When the Portola Expedition camped at the lakes in September 1769, the soldiers killed a bear and feasted on it. Although Father Crespi, diarist and spiritual counselor for the expedition, wanted to call the lake "Lake of the Martyrs San Juan de Perucia and San Pedro de Sacro Terrato," the soldiers' more humble name of Oso Flaco, or "lean bear," stuck.

You'll cross a bridge over the placid lake waters, then follow a long wooden boardwalk toward the dunes. The trail tops a dune

crest and offers fine coastal views from the bold headland above
Avila Beach south to Point Sal.

Walk down the dunes to water's edge and head south. Three
miles of beach walking brings you to the Santa Maria River.
Among the many native and migratory waterfowl residing at the
river mouth are the California least tern and the California brown
pelican. Across the river is Rancho Guadalupe County Park and the
highest sand dune on the west coast, 450-foot-tall Mussel Rock.

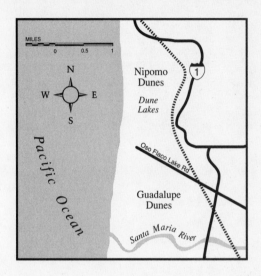

Information Sources

The Parks

Andrew Molera State Park
Big Sur Station, #1
Big Sur, CA 93920
(408) 624–7195

Año Nuevo State Reserve
Pescadero, CA 94060
(415) 879–2025

Asilomar State Beach
c/o Monterey District
(408) 384–7695

Big Basin Redwoods State Park
21600 Big Basin Way
Boulder Creek, CA 95006
(408) 338–6132

Big Sur Multi-Agency Information
(408) 667–2315

Burleigh Murray Ranch State Park
c/o Bay Area District
250 Executive Park Boulevard, Suite 4900
San Francisco, CA 94134
(415) 330–6300

Butano State Park
1500 Cloverdale Road, Box 3
Pescadero, CA 94060
(415) 874–0173

Carmel River State Beach
c/o Monterey District
(408) 667–2315

Castle Rock State Park
15000 Skyline Boulevard
Los Gatos, CA 95030
(408) 867–2952

Elkhorn Slough National Estuarine Sanctuary
(408) 633–2461

Fitgerald Marine Reserve
P.O. Box 451
Moss Beach, CA 94038
(415) 728–3584

Forest of Nisene Marks State Park
c/o Sunset State Beach
201 Sunset Beach Road
Watsonville, CA 95076
(408) 724–1266

Garrapata State Park
Big Sur Station, #1
Big Sur, CA 93920
(408) 624–7195

Hearst San Simeon State Historical Monument
P.O. Box 8
San Simeon, CA 93452
MISTIX (800) 444–4445 for tour reservations

Henry Cowell Redwoods State Park
c/o Santa Cruz District
(408) 335–4598

Julia Pfeiffer Burns State Park
Big Sur Station, #1
Big Sur, CA 93920
(408) 624–7195

Lake San Antonio County Park
P.O. Box 2620
Bradley, CA 93426
(805) 472–2311

Los Padres National Forest

Main office:
6144 Calle Real
Goleta, CA 93117
(805) 683–6711

Monterey Ranger District:
406 South Mildred
King City, CA 93930
(408) 385–5434

Santa Lucia Ranger District:
1616 Carlotti Drive
Santa Maria, CA 93454
(805) 925–9538

McNee Ranch State Park
c/o Bay Area District
(415) 330–6300

Midpeninsula Regional Open Space District
330 Distel Drive
Los Altos, CA 94022
(415) 691–1200

Montana de Oro State Park
Los Osos, CA 93402
(805) 528–0513

Monterey State Historic Park
#20 Custom House Plaza
Monterey, CA 93940
(408) 649–7118

Morro Bay State Park
Morro Bay, CA 93442
(805) 772–2560

Natural Bridges State Beach
c/o Santa Cruz District
(408) 423–4609

Pfeiffer Big Sur State Park
Big Sur Station, #1
Big Sur, CA 93920
(408) 667–0191

Pismo State Beach
(805) 489–2684

Point Lobos State Reserve
Route 1, Box 62
Carmel, CA 93923
(408) 624–4909

Point Sur State Historic Park
(408) 625–4419, 667–2316

Portola State Park
Route 2, Box F
La Honda, CA 94020
(415) 948–9098

Salinas River State Beach
(408) 384–7695

Sam McDonald County Park
c/o San Mateo County Parks Department
(415) 879–0238

San Mateo County Park and Recreation Department
590 Hamilton Street
Redwood City, CA 94063
(415) 879–0238

San Pedro County Park
600 Oddstad Boulevard
Pacifica, CA 94044
(415) 355–8289

Wilder Ranch State Historic Park
c/o Santa Cruz District
(408) 688–3241

California State Park District Offices

Often, individual state parks are hard to reach by telephone. Staff are usually out in the field—and thus keep irregular office hours. One way to obtain information is to contact district offices, each of which usually administers several parks in a particular area. Sometimes the first person who answers the phone is quite helpful, sometimes not, but if you're persistent you'll usually get an answer to your questions.

Bay Area District
250 Executive Park Boulevard, Suite 4900
San Francisco, CA 94134
(415) 330–6300

Monterey District
2211 Garden Road
Monterey, CA 93940
(408) 649–2836

San Luis Obispo Coast District
3220 S. Higuera Street, #311
San Luis Obispo, CA 93401
(805) 549–3312

San Simeon District
Hearst San Simeon State Historical Monument
750 Hearst Castle Road
San Simeon, CA 93452
(805) 927–2020

Santa Cruz District
101 Madeline Drive
Aptos, CA 95003
(408) 688–3241

Index